THE
$\mathcal{I}$NVITATION

THE INVITATION

A Memoir of Family Love and Reconciliation

JOAN HAGGERTY

Douglas & McIntyre
Vancouver/Toronto

To Thomas

94 95 96 97 98   5 4 3 2 1

Douglas & McIntyre
1615 Venables Street
Vancouver, British Columbia
V5L 2H1

Canadian Cataloguing in Publication Data

Haggerty, Joan.
  The invitation
  ISBN 1-55054-097-1
  1. Haggerty, Joan—Family. 2. Authors, Canadian (English)—20th century—Family relationships. I. Title.
PS8565.A35Z53 1994   C818'.5403   C94-910045-5
PR9199.3.H33Z468 1994

Editing by Robert Amussen and Barbara Pulling
Cover and text design by Rose Cowles
Cover photograph by Armelle Bigot
Typeset by Vancouver Desktop Publishing Centre
Printed and bound in Canada by D. W. Friesen and Sons Ltd.
Printed on acid-free paper ∞

ONE

1

I hadn't seen Sean since he was six weeks old when the invitation to his coming of age party arrived from France. He's the second of my three children, born thirteen months after Sophie, my eldest. Sean went to live with the Richters in Paris when he was ten days old; at the time, I was living in England, working in London as a free-lance artist in the schools.

The invitation was actually sent to Sophie. I'd just driven back from a sketching trip, and the airmail envelope with her name on it was lying on the mat below the mail slot. We lived at the top of a hill above city hall in Vancouver in a comfortable old duplex, badly in need of paint, with rambling rooms and good mouldings. The house stuck up above the stucco bungalows lining the rest of the block, and some said it looked like an old ship about to career off into the Pacific. The fire escape stairs were tacked on the front and led up to a small platform like a crow's-nest that the neighbourhood kids loved. From there, you could look out across the inlet to the folding blue north shore mountains and the outer islands.

Sophie often had letters from the Richters—she'd gone over to visit twice, once with friends of ours when she was thirteen and once when she was seventeen, and since then she had kept in touch with her brother. I slipped the envelope into my purse to deliver on the way back from the family cottage where I was going that evening to work on some murals. Luke, my thirteen-year-old son, was coming with me. He didn't have any friends on Bowen Island; he had more up the coast where we used to live but he came over to Bowen with me sometimes if his friends in town were busy or he felt like sleeping. He liked to read comics but occasionally regressed and went down to the beach to turn over stones and look at crabs for a while. Luke knew who Sean was, sort of; we'd always had the pictures and letters, but it didn't mean too much to him yet.

At the cottage, we settled down early, and I took the unopened letter out of my purse and put it on the bedside table beside my mom's bed where I slept. When I woke in the night, I touched it to make sure it was still there. Lately, a deer had been hanging around the point; its steady munching woke me up, and when I leaned out the window, it was eating our hydrangeas in the moonlight, its mouth working over the paperish blue flowers dangling on either side of its lips. I clapped my hands to chase it away; it bounded off into the forest harder on its feet than you'd think, more rigid, not at all like the stag at eve.

In the morning the tide was in, the water gliding off in two directions at once; the silver current edged into the open channel and the green track pulled back towards the rocks below the house. A whole party of tiny lights danced in the forest I could see through the kitchen window, a cluster that would emerge from behind the trees as the Langdale ferry blinking and shining its way up behind the dark islands of Keats and Gambier.

A tugboat strained forward, then the *yowyowyowyow* of the sea gulls as they swooped into view against the bank of trees; the tug was too far away for me to see the towline, and when the barge of peaked sawdust finally appeared from behind the bluff edging our beach, it seemed to be on its own.

Luke came from the back bedroom into the old yellow tongue-and-groove kitchen as I warmed the milk for the coffee and cocoa, dark hair hanging over his eyes, his stocky body still thick from sleep. I poured his cocoa into one of the china mugs that had been there as long as I could remember; he picked out the blodge of skin with a spoon. Sophie would hate that. He stared at the half grapefruit on the cutting board.

"Is this for me?"

"Sure. Are you going to cut it?"

"Maybe I'll just squeeze it." He sat down with his hair in his eyes and turned his attention to his porridge.

I put in a morning's work on my painting, then put my supplies away. "We'd better get back to town. I have this letter to take to Sophie."

"We have to. I have a game anyway."

A game meant soccer or baseball, this time baseball. He picked up his glove from the chair beside him and started pounding his ball into it, over and over again.

Tall Douglas fir grew in the yard; two of them stood like giant gateposts to the road on the narrow point of land, a thumb stretching away to the cove where the ferry dock webbed out to the index finger. Slopes of cedar and fir dropped straight down to the water. The lower branches of the trees had fallen off years ago, leaving an expanse of trunk before the upper limbs began. We stood on the ferry being blown by the wind. Another tug and barge passed, this time transporting logs. The gulls turned and flew straight at us so we could see through their wings.

I drove Luke to his game, watched him play in his determined way, then left for Chinatown and the house where Sophie had moved in with her boyfriend, Gresco. It looked more like a fort they'd thrown up overnight on the edge of an empty lot than it did a house. The old clapboard siding was painted mole-brown and so were the windowpanes; Sophie and Gresco had banged the gaps in the siding together with nails and plywood and hung a variety of objects on the outside walls. Snowshoes crossed neatly under the broken back window. Pots and pans hung by strings on the door to double as knockers. The bramble-covered back seat of Gresco's castoff van blocked the doorway, and I had to lean over it and rap a frying pan against the scarred door to announce myself. Sophie came right away, as if afraid the door might collapse under the knocking. She flicked her blonde bangs out of her eyes. Her fingernails were buffed pearl, but her feet were unspeakable. Whenever we were going away for the weekend and there might be a dinner, I'd suggest she bring a dress and she'd bring one, but trailing it behind her by the collar. This time she had her old trench coat on. She'd had to figure out something, she said, because there were so many people coming by all the time and she had her privacy to consider. If it was someone she didn't want to see at the door, she said she was on her way out. If it was someone she did want to see, she could tell them to come right in. She stood there in the sunlight squinting at the envelope and I wondered, as I have so often, what it must be like to know a brother your mother has never met. "Come on in, Mom." She clutched the letter to the shelter of her chest and turned back into the kitchen. "What's the fellow doing? I told him I don't live at home any more. I gave him the address, too. Why'd he send it to your place?"

She looked at me as if I ought to know, then crossed back over the linoleum floor painted pitch black on top of the dirt. I'd suggested it could be quite nice with some new linoleum but no, she said, it had to stay like that so Gresco's band could drag their heavy sound equipment across it. With all the windows painted over, there was no light, and every surface was littered with newspapers and overflowing ashtrays. The blender on the arborite counter didn't appear to have anything in it, but it jumped around as if on a short circuit. She pulled out the plug absent-mindedly, first jerking it a couple of times like a small pet on a leash, then sat cross-legged on the plastic and chrome kitchen chair and slit the envelope with a buttered table knife. Her hands were elegant, narrow and thin-boned.

"Oh, don't sit there, Mom. That's the gismo we're using to fix the electric meter. Gresco knows how to make it run backwards every third day."

"Oh Sophie."

"Oh Sophie yourself. Where's Luke?"

"He has a game."

"Ah."

I moved a ceramic panther off another chair so I could sit down. Everything had been left exposed—the bricks, the insulation. Higher up, a canoe hung in the eaves along with what looked like bunches of dried tansy.

"They're having a party for Sean. He sends kisses. *Gros baisers à Kathleen*, it says here."

"Really?"

"Yes, look."

The printed buff paper showed a drawing of some mediaeval people, some on foot, some on horseback, some carrying banners and laurels, all of them wandering along a path to the edge of the page. A gothic alphabet decorated the other side, oak trees twisted into the shapes of letters. Sophie read, translating from the French. *Welcome, heroes and heroines of all history. Come down from Olympus, come out of your forests, away from your huts and put on your holiday clothes. Come in your multitudes, magicians, fairies, enchanters and enchantresses, be honoured guests for the evening as we celebrate the coming of age of young Prince Sean Thomas. Bring him philtres, powders, talismans and sparkling wishes, and taste with us the magical air of Pruniers and help us celebrate the summer solstice . . .*

She laughed. "God, Mother, it'll be insane. A bunch of loonies fopping around the corridors. You should go."

"Me? I couldn't go."

"Why not? Luke's going to camp. You could charge it."

"Don't be silly, Sophie."

"All right, it's just an idea. You don't have to get thin-nostrilled about it. I'm going to the store for milk." She flipped the invitation up in the air like a magician's hanky; my eyes followed it as if tracking a mosquito until it settled back on the table. She went upstairs to get some change.

"What's all this on the other side?"

"I don't know. Ideas for costumes maybe."

Aladin, Blanche-Neige, Cendrillon, Didon, Éros, Finette, Gargantua, Hercule, Icare, Jason, King Kong, l'Oiseau bleu, Melusine, Narcisse, Orphée. Cet abécédaire n'est qu'un aide-mémoire; souvenez-vous, ils sont mille et mille, ces personnages fabuleux des contes et légendes qui nous ont tant charmés, effrayés, émerveillés . . . Choisissez celui que vous aimez le mieux et prenez-en l'apparence.

"Your accent's not bad, Mom."

"My accent's terrible. What does *effrayer* mean?"

"To frighten. Who have frightened us."

"Oh."

My hands were shaking as I put some water in the kettle. I called up to her. "Sophie, are you sure you want to stay here? You and Gresco could have the upstairs bedroom at home . . ."

She glared at me from the trap door at the top of the stairs. The staircase was bagged underneath with green plastic to keep dirt from people's shoes from falling down onto the kitchen counter.

There were some stale bran muffins in the bread box and butter in the side tray of the fridge. *Le Petit Poucet, Quasimodo, Robin des bois, La petite sirène, Tristan, Ulysse . . . Le Petit Poucet.* I found her French dictionary leaning beside the paperback Colette she used to read curled up on her bed back in the days when she would spend hours drawing rainbows in the margins of her exercise books. What do they call it, the latency period? And cats. Always cats. *Poucet.* Tom Thumb. *Blanche.* White. *Neige.* Snow.

Sophie and Luke. Two children, but with Sean's ghost trailing behind them as they walked down forest trails. Sometimes I thought I could see his outline, but the rest of him stayed transparent, as if sculpted in ice. Once, I hesitantly sent him a card of an arctic iceberg, the transparent greens and turquoises soft around the edges. Token gestures, trying to stay on the sidelines as if there was any place for me in his life, his family situation; there wasn't, never had been, never would be. Sometimes keeping his existence under wraps felt like screaming at the same time I was whispering, as in a dream, where people were straining to hear me when I was shouting as loud as I could but they kept telling me to speak up.

It was the end of summer eighteen years earlier in Formentera, Spain, and Sophie wasn't walking yet. I'd gone ahead from London to find Andrew and Sophie and me a place to stay for our holidays. The landlord had pigs that squealed through the hot nights; in the morning, he fed them scraps of food from the local restaurant. I lay in bed, Sophie's cot beside mine in the white room, my hand on Sean in my belly, staring at the ceiling, wide awake all night. When I rented the place, I told them my husband would be joining us, but they looked as if they knew perfectly well he wouldn't come. I went to the bar they called the Fonda every day to look for Andrew's letter telling us he was on his way. I put Sophie in her stroller and we bumped over the rough trail every day to the beach, Sean inside me riding high and kicking hard.

Unprotected and exposed, far from home, I had come to Europe two years previously looking for home. We weren't backpacking—it was earlier than that—but we were looking for the authentic European experience. We'd read so much about it, and the hip professors at the university kept telling us we ought to go and get some real culture under our belts. They used that kind of casual language so we would take them seriously. I'd met Andrew at the University of British Columbia Players' Club. Black clothes were in. So was depression. Appearing cheerful was out. He sat at the first table in the cafeteria under the old auditorium, sullen and preoccupied. We talked about existentialism, about Sartre and Beckett and Genet. The university peninsula is bordered by Wreck Beach where nowadays people swim naked, but no one swam nude back then.

We hitchhiked across Canada, took a freighter to Liverpool, were married in London, and spent the season going to plays, paying two shillings and sixpence to sit in the gods. We saw John Gielgud's Hamlet and Peter O'Toole's Hamlet all in one week. Then Andrew got a job up north in a weekly repertory company where the actors performed one play in the evenings and prepared the following week's play in the afternoons. I was miserable from the day I joined him. The unthinkable had happened; he had met someone else, an actress in the company. I arrived looking radiant, he said, in a new cape I'd made evenings in the bed-sitter where I'd moved after we'd given up our flat. I'd stayed in London so I could finish a month or so more of the work I was doing at a school where I was teaching. The actress was sitting on his bed wearing one of his T-shirts. At night in the narrow bed with its ornate headboard he said he'd never really thought of himself as married, he was more or less taking it month by month. I got pregnant with Sophie soon after that, but he left to be with Alison so I went home to my parents in Vancouver to wait for my daughter to be born. I missed him so much, I felt turned inside out. In spite of everything, I wanted him to see Sophie, Sophie to see him. Back in university days, I had sent him a note: *I want to be as close to you as the wet skirt of a salt girl to her body. I think of you always.* A poem I had read somewhere. After Sophie was born, he wrote to me, would I like to try again? We could spend the winter in Ibiza. The affair was over. Everyone told me not to go, my family, my friends, but I talked myself into thinking it was for the best. He would change, I told them, he just didn't want to feel tied down. Sophie needed her father. At the time it didn't occur to me that I was closing down my options, eliminating the possibility of coming back to Vancouver if I got into difficulty again.

Andrew and Sophie and I hadn't been in Spain more than a couple of months when he was off again. Someone wrote him about a part in a show. He would find us a new flat in London, he said; it would be good for the baby to stay in the sun. He would send for me. He liked the baby very much.

We were in an apartment by the sea with a red tile floor and I had started to paint again, sketching every morning with Sophie propped on three pillows staring out the window at the sea. It was lonely. Andrew seemed to find it so easy, sleeping with other people. It made me feel sick, the idea of him with someone else, let alone me doing it, but I found myself thinking maybe I'd be more attractive to him if I were less needy, if I had the air of having other options the way he did. It was as if we were operating on the minus side of zero, in a different world where you were aware of your waist only as a place for your lover to slip his hand. Bending over backwards to adjust to whatever would make you desirable. I didn't really think it would happen—I felt so bonded to him through Sophie's face and skin—but the thought of it as a strategy occurred to me.

And then one day I went to an opening at a gallery behind the local café and found myself more interested in the man who was landscaping the stones in front of the gallery than in the touristy paintings. I sat in the shade with my camera watching the way he worked; he was absorbed in what seemed to be a casual arrangement of stones around various cactus and bougainvillea plants. The result seemed to please him, and I saw that what he had done was to separate the smallest stones, pebbles really, from the area of slightly larger stones down a small slope where more plants were embedded. He then slid the largest ones into the flat area at the bottom as if they had passed through a series of graduated sieves. The bougainvillea sloped down a trellised walk.

He had blue-black hair pushed back and there was a kind of sweetness around his eyes. I liked his slight way of being in the world, his air of taking up his share of space yet concentrating his energy on the task at hand. The high flat planes of his forehead seemed almost Tsimshian; he certainly wasn't Spanish. I wondered where he came from, how he got there.

One of my passions at the time was photographing gardens, and the light in the heat of the day there contrasted with the sharp line of shade from the angle of the gallery roof and his aquiline nose in profile; I liked the idea of how the contrast would register in black and white. He looked up once as the shutter clicked—he wasn't tall—

glanced at me briefly and then back at the large white leafless crocus he was slipping into the ground. I was attracted to him in part by the self-contained way he had about him, almost wanting to get on the inside to see how he did it. He would know the exact moment to look aside when he stood to lose his self-respect. I put my camera back in the long-handled straw basket I carried Sophie in and took a chance that he spoke English.

"I hope you don't mind," I said. "It's nice, this area you're making."

He came over to where I was sitting to see the effect from there. "Yeah, it's not bad." The sun made the stone work flatter and flatter. The gallery was on a hill with a steep drop to the ocean and the afternoon promised to be hot and still. He smiled down at me.

"Have you got a baby in there?"

Sophie smiled back, broadly as usual, showing her general pleasure at being in the world.

"Is this your gallery?"

"No, I'm just doing the garden."

He gestured to his van, which I could see was loaded with tools and camping equipment, even a portable drafting board. Bryce Wilson, Landscape Architect, was written on the side panel.

He was from L.A., spent winters in Baja where he lived on the beach out of the back of another van he kept over there and cooked fish wrapped in corn husks. The colours of the fish down there were something to see, he said. One fish was blue when he caught it; the minute it came out of the water it turned black and then it turned green. We talked about light and gardens and enjoyed comfortable stretches when we talked about nothing at all. The still afternoon passed into evening, which he told me he wanted to spend on a hill back of the town because it was a good place to watch the flash of green light that zipped into focus when the sun slid over the hill.

"Flash of green light?"

"Yeah. It happens just the instant the sun disappears over the horizon. You have to wait and look for it. Not many people see it, but it happens every night. My uncle showed me when I was a kid."

Sophie and I went with him, sat on the hill and waited for the flash of green light, which he said he saw but I didn't think ever appeared. I liked him but took the next steps more rapidly than I would have normally, even if I hadn't been married. It was as if my uncertainty about Andrew threw my form into a concave shape and I needed the clear sweet desire that Bryce showed me that night to lift me once again out of clay, so I knew where I ended and the air began. Because he wanted me I felt alive. *Blanche-Neige* here, not Beauty and the Beast.

I only spent one night with him; he had finished his job at the gallery and was leaving the next day. He passed through my life, the agent for Sean's future, although neither of us could have known that at the time. Niki would call him the Blackfoot.

Eventually Andrew did send for us and met us at Waterloo Station, where we caught a train to Sheffield to visit his mother for the weekend. Sitting in the damp club car, I felt guilty. Later on in the trip I told him, wanting to be honest, and as a way of seeking absolution, thinking that if I told him, the incident would be cancelled out and put us back on neutral ground, make us even. What made me think that an admission would be in anyone's interest? That

I could have it both ways? Keeping it to myself would have given me that advantage of knowing I could reach out to someone else, was capable of that. But I blurted it out, denying myself privacy and respect. He looked out the window and his mouth worked slowly. He didn't get upset the way I did when he told me of his forays.

"I felt . . . ugly after being pregnant. I wanted someone to show me I wasn't. It's more like *you* have to . . . or something."

"I don't have to," he laughed. We lifted the stroller off the train and spent the middle of the month in the back bedroom of his mother's house in Sheffield. We walked with Sophie on the fields at the edge of town and ate Sunday lunches of mutton and thick custard.

But at the end of the month, back in London in a Bennington Gardens flat I had been painting and decorating, my breasts were sore and I was nauseated. I went to the clinic and had a pregnancy test, but it was negative. Weeks later, when I still felt pregnant, I went back, and this time it came out positive, the nurse explaining that the first test must have been taken too early.

"No one even mentioned that as a possibility," I said in alarm.

"It could have been a mistake."

"A mistake?"

"They do happen."

The blood drained from my face when I told Andrew, sitting at the kitchen table with a calendar counting the days. He had come in cheery from a cast party. I waited until he had sat down with a drink.

"Andrew, I'm pregnant. They said the other test was too early."

"No, you're not."

"Pardon? No, really. The . . . other . . . was such a remote possibility. I still had a bit of period. Chances are . . ."

"Oh, chances," he said. "Never mind. It'll be all right."

But of course it wasn't all right and I knew it now eight months later standing in the middle of the hot road outside the Fonda, my hair flaming, reading the letter again and again saying he wasn't coming to Spain. Sean's clenched fist pounded me inside. It was probably the fear and insecurity that brought on the premature labour early the next morning. Friends I'd met at Mitjorn Beach arranged for me to go to Ibiza from Formentera; they would look after Sophie. Two of the local men who had a boat took me over; it was rough in the channel on the two-hour crossing and I lay in a berth trying to remember my breathing and reassuring them that the contractions weren't strong, that it was probably just the type of pre-labour I'd experienced with Sophie.

The back seat of the taxi I got into at the quay in Ibiza didn't seem to have any springs. After ten minutes, we pulled up in front of a large handsome villa with latticework that was now a clinic. There were shutters on the windows and it was cooled by the dappled shade of plane trees. None of the staff used rubber gloves. The end piece of the speculum they brought in seemed big enough for a horse. They examined me, patted me in an offhand way and a few minutes later brought in a woman from the delivery room and put her in the bed next to mine. Both our beds were draped in mosquito netting hung from circular wire frames in the ceiling, but they didn't pull the curtains across. I could see everything that was going on.

A doctor with black hair slicked back with pomade pushed her legs open, drew her labia up smartly between his second and third fingers as if sewing up a bird for the oven. Just as he was about to begin to stitch, he stopped with the needle poised over her crotch and asked the nurse if the afterbirth was out yet. He started his work, but the woman kept pushing his hands away and he grew more and more irritated.

"Stop," she said. "That hurts."

The amazing thing was, he did. Exasperated, he snapped his bag shut and left her there, a long piece of black thread trailing down her leg. Once he left, she turned to me, almost embarrassed at having gotten her way.

"I think you're going to have to let him finish," I whispered in Spanish.

"He's gone."

"Well, yes."

"I want my baby." She started to cry. The room was hot with bits of dust in the shafts of light; it smelt of the doctor's pomade and lemon toilet water. It felt like a recovery room in any hospital in any country where they take the baby away to fingerprint it or whatever it is they do, when all your instincts are screaming to bond and they have the power to return or not return whenever they see fit. I reached across for her hand. "It'll be okay. They'll bring him in a minute. Is it a boy?" She nodded and smiled.

When they finally brought him in, all bundled up, and handed him to her, she forgot about me.

My labour seemed to have stopped. I sent a message with a taxi driver to the driver of the boat, who would give it to another taxi driver on Formentera. The request was for my friends to pick up our packed stuff at the apartment and bring Sophie to Ibiza. Late that afternoon, I swung my legs over the side of the bed, took off the hospital gown, folded it neatly, put my arms up through the yoke of my pale-yellow and green striped cotton sun dress with the singlet top and wide skirts from the armpits down. At least I was tanned. I would go to London. Managing to board the plane might be tricky but I had to get to the safety of the British medical system. I had finally realized that Andrew wasn't going to change; my construct had been wishful thinking and I was going to need all the safety I could get. I'd had a lot of false labour with Sophie and figured I knew what I was doing. I stopped at the receptionist to pay my account, put on my sunglasses, left the hospital and sashayed as best I could between the tables at the café where I'd arranged to meet my friends. They were a mild-mannered couple from Islington who lived on bulgur wheat and hope. We'd met because they had a daughter, Raphael, who was Sophie's age.

"Hey, I owe you one," I said gratefully as I sat down.

"Don't worry about it. We were coming over to Ibiza today anyway. Just get yourselves home safely."

"Thanks." Sophie climbed into my lap while I drank a soda water and then we left for the airport.

In Palma, waiting to change planes, the contractions started again, but I had no choice except to board. I folded the stroller and handed it to the flight attendant. She looked at me and raised her eyebrows but I willed her to silence. Breathe, I told myself. Don't forget to breathe. The flight attendant reappeared, a concerned look on her face, with a colouring book and crayons for Sophie. Fold down this tray, Sophie, that's a good girl. The skin on my belly was tight, like a drum. Sean waved from inside like a marooned sailor. Then the announcement came that we would be landing shortly and we should please fasten our seat belts. Mine wasn't long enough; I tried it over the top, underneath. We have to put the trays up now, Sophie. No, *up*. Breathe. Sophie, you can take the colouring book. We'll put it in your bag.

"Nurse, excuse me, I mean stewardess, I don't want to alarm anyone, but do you have ground contact from here? Is it possible to radio ahead for an ambulance?"

"An ambulance? Are you all right?"

"Just."

"How far apart are they?"

"It's not . . . it's how long they are, but never mind, just . . ."

At Heathrow the ambulance was waiting with two grinning, cheerful attendants. I told them we had to go to St. Mary's, Paddington, but first to stop at 15 Bennington Gardens so my husband could take Sophie. Looking up at the windows when we pulled up, I could tell by the soft light that Andrew had candles in wine bottles in the front room of the flat. He bounded down to the street, throwing his black hair off his translucent white forehead. *Sophie must be scared. Musn't frighten her. Gently. This is too important for anger. We need him.* He lifted Sophie out of the back of the van as the paramedics distracted me with a shot of morphine. He said he would come to the hospital in the morning. They slammed the back doors and we left for the hospital down the street. You're going to be all right. They kept saying that.

The next morning I told the nurses it could go on like

this for quite a while, you never knew. I was cheerful, relieved to be safe. I'd almost persuaded them to break down and give me an egg, teasing them; they were going to give me bangers for breakfast, good old England. The door opened and Andrew slipped in. He closed it gently with his other palm and came over to stand stiffly by the side of the bed, slim, gently hesitant, black turtleneck sweater, slim trousers, banker's shoes.

"They want me to get up and walk. I think he's a boy, a kind of quiet boy like you. Why didn't you come? I was waiting for you. I had a place and everything." I tried to hold his eyes, but he kept looking at the floor.

"Who's looking after Sophie?"

"She's at the flat."

"Who's looking after her?"

"Niki."

"Who's Niki?"

"A Dutch girl, she's been staying at the flat. She's with some other people from Amsterdam."

"Is she nice? Is she responsible?"

"Of course she's nice. Of course she's responsible. Why wouldn't she be?"

"Why didn't you come to Spain?"

He looked at the floor again. "That's not my baby."

I should have known. *Play dead.*

"Andrew, we talked about this. I still had a bit of a period. I wouldn't have slept with him otherwise. We had this all worked out."

"You shouldn't have."

I looked frantically from side to side. They'd shaved me; the stubble scratched against my nightie.

"Andrew, not now, please. I can't handle this right now. I understand how you feel but not now."

"You're just saying that."

"I'm not just saying that."

Stall. "Will you get the nurse, please?"

When the nurse came in, he looked cross, as if she had interfered with his kill. She waddled me into the cubicle in my terry-cloth dressing gown and paper slippers and I held onto both her arms as she lowered me onto the toilet. I kept holding on, but she pried my hands off one by one. I sat there cleaning the fingernails of one hand with my other index finger. When we came back he was sitting on the chair where I left him. The nurse left me leaning against the edge of the bed.

"You did more than me," he said and made no move to help me as I levered myself back up on the bed.

"I did what?"

"Had it all worked out. I changed my mind while you were away."

"You changed your mind?" Panic set in under my skull ready to blow off the top of my head. "Just because *you* can't get pregnant."

"What if I could? Would you want to be looking at some other woman's face staring up at you every damn day?"

"It won't be like that."

"How do you know?"

"I just know."

"Niki will look after Sophie. I've given her some money. I'll send more."

"Where are you going?"

"To Newcastle. I have work there."

"Please don't do this. Please don't go now."

"I'm going tomorrow, actually."

"You're going tomorrow?" I turned to the wall. If I hadn't come home yesterday, he would have been gone, that's what he was telling me. Someone called Niki would have been there.

"This is an excuse, isn't it? You'd have left again anyway."

"No, it's not an excuse."

I decided to take a long shot and call his bluff.

"If that's what you're going to do, Andrew, I guess you'd better leave and let me have my breakfast. I have a feeling I'm going to need it."

And the amazing thing was, he did.

Lie, squat, crouch. Do whatever you want. Whatever is comfortable. They rolled me onto a wide table and the labour came down fast and hard. Sean arched his back like a gentleman, bunched out fast and furious, scrambled up in front of my eyes so fast I hardly had time to lean over and catch him under the armpits before he would have been up the wall above me like a squirrel. A baby, I announced, astonished, as he kept on coming out. How could he have been inside me? Hands and feet and eyes and swollen genitals and wide open mouth. He was up over me in the air but there was no father there to receive him. No husband up over top of me telling me he was crowning, the colour of his hair—it should have been mixed with mine. No one putting their knuckle between his gums and hooking him out in his thin silver wrapping, tucking a hand under his folded leather bum and holding him like a leprechaun. There was too much air between us. I couldn't find him. I kept pulling it back like yards of transparent cloth, and the more I pulled, the more I got tangled up. They brought him back and the nurses laughed. What did you think he was going to be, mother, an elephant? Well, no, I hadn't thought that. He wasn't a baby until I saw him coming out of me that fast. When they put him up beside my face, I was sure from the feel of his skin and the narrow line of blue behind his translucent eyelids and the bits of saliva at the corners of his mouth that he was Andrew's baby. Part of me wanted to wire him to come home, as if the hurricane had missed the house after all. As quickly as the nurses and doctors came, they carried the baby off. They turned out the lights, packed up and went home. They had no idea I was alone.

I cried that night, worrying about Sophie at home, feeling flat and weak and rejected. All the plans and hopes I had had for the family were blown sky high, our bonds broken and scattered: Sean down in the nursery, not Andrew's because Andrew said he wasn't, Sophie at the flat being looked after by someone I didn't know, me devastated and alone in this bed, him God knows where, heading north again. When I finally fell asleep, I dreamt of swimming to try to get to the children who were stranded on separate rocks, but they were the wrong ones. The wrong children. Everything was one-dimensional; none of us had arms or voices. I woke up feeling as isolated as if I were in jail.

When they brought Sean to me from the nursery I cried again. He had the small distinguished face of a miniature statesman: the dignified nose, skin pulled tight over his cheekbones, his forehead a walnut. I touched his fine cheek with my fingertip and tried to nurse him, but the milk wasn't in yet, just the yellow fluid, and it hurt pulling down my breasts, spokes to the hub of my nipples. A few minutes later, a hospital clerk yanked the curtain back from my bed and stood with her pencil over her clipboard. The sunlight glared as I squinted up at her.

"I'm taking care of a few formalities this morning, mother. We'll need a birth certificate for your baby. Could you tell me baby Sean's last name? His father's name?"

"There is no father. This baby doesn't have a father."

"You don't have to be melodramatic, mother."

"I'm not being melodramatic. Do you see one anywhere around here? Under the bed?"

A nurse came in with lunch; the toast was made of cotton wool. Buses lurched by on the street, squeezed by the cars on either side. My own dad would be sitting now in the living room chair in their house in Vancouver, staring without blinking at the wall.

"Excuse me, mother, there has to be one, even if it's just biological." She finally left, as exasperated as the doctor in Ibiza had been.

That afternoon Niki came to the hospital. I had no idea who she was when she came into the room. She just walked in and stood at the foot of the bed holding onto the railing, smiling, her face scarred from acne, a kind of artificial alertness about her. She wore a bandanna tied around her forehead and hooped earrings. Like most Dutch girls she spoke several languages. All over Europe in those days, we stayed in other people's flats and people stayed in our flat. You'd come home to find a stranger there who said he was a friend of a friend. Fine. Except that it wasn't. People got the clap. The women got PID. Everyone picked up everyone else in their Volkswagen vans and people pretended to know each other before they really did. There was a kind of haze that obliterated real differences. Everyone was walking around in multiple exposure. If we could have seen our brazen giddiness for what it was we would have been embarrassed, but at the time it felt as if we shared an innocent collective secret. You'd walk down a road in any one of a number of cities and smile when you recognized that the stoned person you were passing on the road was also walking four inches above the ground. You'd nod and say, "Really?"

"Really."

It was daft, but we liked it. The question now was the price.

Niki behaved as if she were part of the camouflage. She had a shield over her face like a mask, a high polish on the veneer—we would have called it her aura—so that access to her was deflected. The bright glint in her eye seemed fixed and would probably stay in place even when she went to sleep. When she woke up, it would still be there like an incandescent sliver.

"Kathleen?"

"Hi."

"I'm Niki."

"Oh. Hi, Niki. Where's Sophie?"

"With Bridget."

"Who's Bridget? I want to go home."

"She's my friend. She's okay. Don't worry."

I didn't think she had slept with Andrew. She seemed too sure of herself. She looked into the cot.

"May I?"

I nodded, turned again to look out the window, wanting Andrew to come rushing through the burning timbers, grab us and say, Everything's okay. It was just a nightmare, we're a family, which would have been true, but instead, here was this Niki person peering in at my son, a swift calculating glance passing across her face.

"Sean doesn't look much like you or Andrew, does he?" she said, touching him, looking at him carefully.

"I don't know."

"The nose, look at the nose."

He was asleep, one fist clenched and thrown back over his head. I loved him whatever they said. It was the way his chin stuck up in the air, barely there, but there.

"That's my nose."

Many people in our family have these noses, hardly any bridge and then a straight ridge. A family story has it that once, long ago in Ontario, a man boarded a train only to find another man with the same nose in his assigned seat.

"By your nose, sir," he said, "you should be a Haggerty."

"By your nose, sir, so should you."

And they were.

When I came home from the hospital in a taxi with Sean, Niki and Sophie greeted me at the door as if I'd been away on a business trip. They were nice and clean. I knelt down with Sean in one arm, put my other arm around Sophie and pulled her into my side until she gave way at the waist and relaxed. With my coat still on, I picked her up and the three of us went to sit on the living room bed.

I leaned back into the pillows to let them get the feel of each other. Sean lay on his back between my opened knees and Sophie leaned against my shoulder. I was exhausted, and sat there feeling that I'd been through a hurricane but somehow, with luck and perseverance, had landed back at my own house. I'd painted the wall framing the three arched windows a deep purple blue and the window sills were white enamel. The art deco curtains were patterned in fresh bright purple and green. High ceilings, the second floor of a house in Bayswater. Lots of wood furniture I'd stripped myself.

My stitches wired me together, pulling me hard up the front of my pelvis; a wire drawstring from my crotch jerked me into the narrow windowless cupboard we called a kitchen, where I put a bottle into a pan of hot water. The drawstring propelled me into the large bathroom where I'd set up a screen I'd dragged home from the Portobello Road and covered in the same flowered print as the curtains. While Niki spent her first few minutes alone with both the children, I sat behind it on the toilet listening to the hum of the fridge with my fingers pressed into the sockets of my eyes, still not able to pee. At least they'd taken out the splinter of a catheter.

A wide low-slung push cart for Sophie that we had painted chartreuse and lined with sheepskins stood by the bathtub. The wallpaper was pink with a faint silver stripe. I turned on the tap and ran the water like they'd told me to. At Whitely's department store next door they had thrown out some white straw baskets used in a display. I'd brought them home and left them in the bathroom, where the steam had turned them to pulp. I had thought I might be able to use them at school; I tried to help students combine dialogue, music and painting in a way that made sense to them, and I loved it, but the work wasn't steady. There were no benefits or maternity leave, so I was out of a job.

I pulled down some toilet paper, snapped the elastic of the pouch of the maternity skirt and pushed my hemorrhoids back in with my finger, hoping I wouldn't have to go back to the hospital to get drained. Looked in the mirror. I should get a haircut, I thought, angled smartly along one side of my jaw. I blew my nose. There might be another fifty quid on the way from Newcastle. Then what? I stood in front of the large mirror with a bevelled edge sunk into a turquoise frame, lifted up my arms, wattles starting underneath. The public health nurse I saw before leaving the hospital had told me that postpartum depression made you subject to feelings of inadequacy. I'll say.

Back in the living room, Sophie was pushing down hard on her brother's delicate skull. I picked her up and put her in her highchair. I put on the new Beatles tape, ran water for the dishes, turned off the water, then had to rewind the tape because I had missed the first few bars. Maybe the music would cut the fog of my depression. But it didn't, it made it worse. *You say yes. I say no.* Niki picked up Sophie's spoon and smeared her mouth with fluorescent carrots and mashed Brussels sprouts, wiped her mouth with a facecloth. *You say good-bye. I say hello.* Sophie picked up her milk, poured it on the floor and laughed. She thought it was very funny. Very funny, Sophie. The baby started crying. Wanting another bottle? Not wanting another bottle? Filling up? Too full? Niki stared blankly at the fridge. All Andrew's suits and jackets hanging in the closet looked empty. Once, when we were swimming at Jericho Beach in Vancouver, he dove underwater and came up with his bathing suit on his head. I laughed the way Sophie had when she threw her milk on the floor. I burst into tears standing at the sink.

"Kathleen, look, is there anything I can do? I'll make some tea."

"No, thanks, Niki. It's okay." I was gulping, blowing my nose.

Niki put the kettle on anyway, then dumped the magnetic letters out of their box and began to snap them on the fridge door in an effort to entertain Sophie. Sean continued to cry when I did, tightening under his rib cage, farting and mewling and waving his hands in the air: I could still feel his kicks in my stomach as if he hadn't been born yet. I picked him up and pressed gently on the hard knot under his rib cage.

Using nails, I'd hung a paisley bedspread across an alcove at the end of the hall to make a closet. It was looped back with a sash now. Once when Andrew pulled it back to get his suit out he ripped the fabric.

"Damn it, why does everything in this place have to fall down?"

"Sorry."

But everything else didn't fall down; everything else was very pretty. I dressed Sophie in matching tights, sweaters and corduroy dresses I made myself.

I tried to pull myself together and be polite to Niki. If this was supposed to be a job for her, I didn't know what kind of money we could work out, and I didn't know what arrangements Andrew had made. We'd have to talk about it. I didn't know how much she knew about the situation, either; from what she'd said in the hospital, she must know something. But for now, as I unpacked, I asked her, "Do you have a family over in Amsterdam or somewhere?"

"No, my mother's dead. I can't find my father."

"Oh, I'm sorry."

"My mother died in a Japanese prison camp where I grew up."

"Where you grew up?"

"First four years of my life, yes."

I looked at her. I knew about Japanese prison camps because my uncle had been in one. They told us he had had to eat slugs. We went to the train station to meet him when he came back from the war. We all fell silent when we saw him; nothing was left of him but a bleached rake that had been lying out in the yard all winter. His eyes were glazed over like Niki's. When my mother and aunts tried to kiss him, he looked into the distance as if at faint smoke on the horizon.

"Do you remember much about it?"

"Enough."

"I'll bet."

I imagined barbed wire on a fence, a spoon hidden under her pillow, a speckled enamel bowl with chopped slugs on the dirt floor, a stretch of frozen earth, mucus spilling over her small chapped lips. I looked from one to the other of my children blankly, cupping Sean's head up against my shoulder while Sophie pulled off his blanket and started tugging at his foot. "Niki, I guess we'd better . . . would you mind getting Sophie's crayons? They're in her basket."

"Oh, right."

She jumped down from the stool she was perched on,

opened the cupboard and began digging in the basket where we kept toys.

The next day, determined to make the best of things, I decided to try to get back to some of my own work. I sorted a pile of photo montages, then gave up and took a long slow walk to the store to get some groceries. When I got back, Niki left for the Portobello Road. She returned in a few hours with an old fur coat that she cut really short, too short, so that she had to sew a piece back on for a hem. She bent the rest into a folded boat shape, trying to shape it into a hat.

"Will Andrew be coming back? I sort of have to know because of money and finding another job."

"I understand. What did he tell you?"

She looked up from her hat. "He said something about Sean not being his."

"We're not sure, that's it really. And I'm just not going to be able to pay you, Niki. He said he'd send some money but I'm not going to be able to work for a while and I don't know when he'll send it or about any steady arrangements. You can see, nothing's very stable here."

"I understand. But I'll have to start looking around."

"You can stay here while you do if you want."

"You're sure that's why he left? I mean, he didn't act very married."

While Sophie and Sean had their naps, I looked at the mess in the studio, trying not to hear what she meant. When I was alone, I always knew what should come next in my work, when to go out to the kitchen for a drink of water so that the synapses didn't disconnect, but when other people were around it all got buried and part of me went numb. I knew perfectly well what she meant but I was not going to think about it. My attempts at raised canvases were scattered around me on the floor, pieces of wood pushing up the canvas from underneath. Some were on a small scale like relief maps of mountain ranges; others had armatures, with the white paint spilling down them like structures for a model railway.

I spread out photographs of the rock formations in the bay below the old town in Ibiza, the ones down near the sea. Among the photos were the ones of Bryce I had taken in front of the gallery, before he came to talk to me. I didn't even have an address for him. Niki was looking over my shoulder.

"Who's this?" she asked, picking up the one of him framed against the white stones.

"Bryce. A friend."

She propped it up on the ledge above what had been the paint mixing table and was now the changing table.

"Sean looks just like him." She opened her eyes wide at me.

I looked again. It seemed like she was right. He was too young to tell, really, he was a newborn, but I saw it that way for a minute, the way she saw it.

I left to run the water for Sean's bath. Niki followed and sat on the floor beside me. I needed the bathroom to myself; you couldn't have a bladder this full and not be able to go. She was very intent; why did she care?

"Look at his nose, look at Sean's nose. And Sean's dark, he's got dark skin."

"Maybe all babies have that kind of skin."

"Did Sophie?"

"Well, no, but . . ."

That brittle metallic look came over her again as she left the room, with me bent over and the flesh of the baby all caught up with mine.

Over the next few days all my time was taken up with feeding and getting supplies. It was not just that I'd lost my place in the work. I'd lost the place in my body that knew what the work wanted, because every pore and muscle was consumed with the babies' needs; my pores were their pores, oozing and secreting and extending out into their bones and blood. My blood didn't circulate around my own body any more; it travelled out into theirs and back up into mine.

For the half hour they went down to sleep, I went out of my studio and came in again. Finally, once, trying again, leaning on the door to push off from it, I walked over, grabbed a thin brush out of the bouquet and quickly, just to catch myself by surprise, took another stab at picking out with dark-green paint some of the hundreds of firs that were climbing a hill, painting the shadow side first and then the wild side with pieces of sky cut wide and loose divided by clouds. A bearded figure walking along the beach dragging a chain pointed out that I should be admiring the barge loaded with logs coming into sight this side of the point. Makes a charming sight, he said. Probably the farm people watching the loaded box cars on the way to Auschwitz said the same thing. Admiring the pastoral train passing by on a gentle summer evening. He reminded me of somebody. I couldn't think who. Eventually the water began to open, green ovals from out of the blue, and a sea gull streaked above the dark hill, reversing suddenly to a black fleck where it collided with the sky, exploding back into white as it crossed down over the tree line and dropped to the sea in a weighted dive where emerging blue ovals now rose from the green.

Even if the wind blew the tops off the trees in the winter, I still had to be back there at the cottage sifting water through a sieve to separate the starfish from the clams. My painting started to know that at last as I sank back in again, got up again, combed a burr of hair from my brush out the window in case the gathering throng was waiting for me. That was the signal, back when there was no difference between the real world and the tiny king in his counting house counting out his money. The people quivered like sand fleas, picking their way across the beach between the rocks turreted with barnacles, rushing across the tide flats like spiders in their chariots so they wouldn't get caught by the tide, spinning their wheels where the shells and gravel scraped the water, dashing into the cave behind a large stone until they finally emerged underground into my yard between the roots at the base of the fir. They backed in from the hollow of the tree, elbows first, jerking their horses' heads around, turning slightly in their saddles to beckon to the riders behind them. Once in the safety of my yard, they demanded to be seated under whatever parapet or canopy took their fancy. My lord with the thin bones raised four fingers (the thumb was tucked into the palm), turned and saluted the rest of the entourage. You had to outfit every single one of them, too. There was no getting around it. You just got one decked out in gold threaded velvet when another tapped you on the shoulder turning her foot every which way until you were chasing a dandelion poof around the garden trying to catch it in case another of their company arrived by air.

There was nothing to do but find my mother, who was picking huckleberries—they were so small it took forever to get enough for a pie—but there she was in the sunlit glade on the other side of the cedars in her white apron with the funny poppies blanket-stitched on the pockets. Her socks were rolled low over her running shoes; her hair turned the other way up above her neck. When she swung around, the place where her nose should have been was black. Her eyes crossed looking for it. She flapped her hand at the crow who flew off with it into the trees. Lucky she'd left her crown back on the kitchen table. Uncle Ned said, Gotcher nose. And stuck his thumb between his fingers to show it to you. Never mind he'd put it back. He was never the same, they said. He drank too much and ran a dark grocery store near Courtenay where the goods sat on shelves in the back and gathered dust. He often sat at the kitchen table at the cottage, never mentioned the war but you knew he was fragile, like a piece of china Mother would have preferred to keep in a box, packed in cotton wool.

I told her about the tiny feet waving like minnows, waggling their insteps up and down the length of the outside wall of the cottage wanting shoes like baby birds cawing for worms.

Up in the cress stream bed by the white birches where the forget-me-nots waved tall blue umbrellas, is that where she saw the bleeding heart? No, no, the bleeding heart would be more their size than the ladyslippers. She'd come with me to fetch them—she understood my urgency—and didn't care about leaving the laundry in a wet bunch in the basket under the clothesline stretched from the fir to the cedar. The needles could fall into it for all she cared, and the ferns spring up and the ivy and moss climb up the north side of the trees tall as the bean-stalk. Always a touch of pink first thing in the spring. The salmonberry blossoms in the bushes, the sudden fox-gloves and, in the more open areas, the fireweed between blades of grass.

When I looked up from my work, Niki was standing behind me holding both babies. I glanced at her out of the corner of my eye.

"No," she said finally, after putting Sophie in her play-pen and handing Sean to me, "the closest I have to par-ents are some friends of mine who live in an apartment in Paris up near Montmartre."

I had to stop anyway. I was nearly doubled up from not being able to urinate and would have to go back to the hospital and get them to put the damn catheter back in.

"Do you know them?"

I laughed. "Of course I don't know them. You haven't even said who they are." I sat down and pulled on some maternity trousers, hating the kangeroo pouch but not able to fit into anything else.

"Well, I'll tell you who they are." The same stunned look came into her eyes and she started picking at the carpet. "The wife—her name's Loesic—she's the kind of person who can make you want to eat a piece of fruit just the way she puts it in a bowl. Do you know what I mean?" She mimed this, picking up a piece of empty space and putting it on the edge of the changing table. It would be better if we were on the ground floor, I thought. It would be better if we were in the country. Anywhere where I could get grounded and find some help distributing the weight. "All she needs is a bundle of straw and a pile of stones."

"Who does?"

"Loesic. But don't think she's dreamy, she's not. She's solid as granite. And Jean-Paul, that's her husband? He's an artist and he laughs a lot, and when he laughs, he turns bright red."

"I trust people who blush. Hand me that safety pin, will you please, Niki?"

"And when you go down to Bouchauds, that's their place in the country? You wake up in the morning and she takes you out to her lilac bushes. You have to hold your face way up high"—she tilted hers up to the light bulb— "and then she shakes dew all over your hair and skin." The skin on her face softened and stretched as if she were sunning it after a long winter. I had the sense this was the only moment she could remember when she was happy.

"Sounds exotic. Very French."

"No, everyone in Paris says if anyone should have children it's the Richters, but they can't." She opened her eyes wide, trying not to blink.

"They can't what?"

"Do it. Have kids." She had collected a pile of beads and hats from Petticoat Lane and hung them on the iron hooks of the mirror. She was trying on some of them and said she knew a technique that would help me deepen the shadows below my eyebrow bones. She said some of the women in the prison camp had made a dress for her from the rag that had been her mother's blanket; they'd washed it first in a rain puddle. Her eyes didn't seem to have pupils most of the time. I kept looking for a focus but couldn't find one.

"I want you to let me invite them over."

"Why?"

"Because you've got to meet them. They're really . . . they're special."

"How do you mean? Why do you say that?"

"Because of the way they are."

"That doesn't tell me anything."

She stood in front of the mirror and worked mascara into the tips of her eyelashes.

When I got home from the hospital in the afternoon, relieved, armed with pills that were supposed to reduce the swelling from the labour and let my system work again, Niki kept following me around the flat telling me about these friends. Jean-Paul could help her because he could speak German; she'd found someone who only spoke German who might be able to tell her something about her father and Jean-Paul could translate. She spent the afternoon lying on the living room rug in her bed-spread skirts turning the pages of magazines for Sophie— *Vogue*, *Nova*, *Elle*. Then she set off to the bakery, came back with some blueberry muffins and fed bits to Sophie, teasing her, holding them just out of her reach. Days went by; Niki and I kept everyone afloat but the situation felt temporary somehow, as if we were trying to rehearse without all the cast present.

The next painting was of an empty castle. *Small triangular flags folded three times in the wind. Horses came rushing out, especially when bugles played.* Sophie was quiet at the moment, too quiet. I went into the living room and found her heaping her toys—her soft yellow duck, her pink pig, her striped fish—carefully balancing one on the other on top of Sean in his cradle, her favourite mouse perched on top like a cherry. He gazed at his sister with a trusting look, as if they were playing on the beach and she was burying him in sand. I knelt down and started to take the toys off him one by one but he started to cry, making circles in the air with his hands. The front door buzzer rang and Sophie started to cry too. I picked her up on my hip and then Niki was beside me, taking Sophie from me as I pulled her tights up around her waist. The buzzer was still going as I went to open the door.

And there they were, tall, like Niki said, the two of them standing before me, glowing, their arms full of roses, beefsteak and champagne.

"Hi, come on in," I said, beckoning back with my head to Niki who stood in the middle of the living room holding Sophie, stunned as if she hadn't really believed they were going to come. Then she put Sophie down and rushed to the door where there was a lot of kissing of cheeks and *ça va, ça va.*

The living room bed wasn't made. I started tidying up, pulling up the blanket so they would have a place to sit, but when I came back into the hall, Loesic Richter hadn't moved. She just stood there looking grave and steady, in loose pants and a velour sweatshirt that she would wear the whole time she was there. Leaning against the dresser smoking a cigarette. She had a thick kind face, hair wound around her head in a braid, no make-up.

She narrowed her eyes at me, then hunched her heavy

shoulders and, leaning firmly into a hefty stride, one foot meeting the ground right after the other, marched into the living room and sat down resolutely in my swivel chair, bouncing it a little to test the spring as if she were buying office furniture. The baby started to cry and had to be fed. I picked him up and went to the kitchen to get a bottle.

"Would you like some tea?" The way her gaze seemed to take in everything and the way her feet met the ground struck me, I'm sure unreasonably, as signs of inner strength. I also liked the way she relaxed, uncontrolled, around her large frame. They both seemed to have come from a place in the country where people carried vegetables and eggs into a tile and stone kitchen.

"I have red zinger, almond or Earl Grey."

Jean-Paul sat down awkwardly on the wrecked chaise longue, his clasped hands dropped between his knees. Lengths of green velvet hung from the chaise where I'd been covering it. He looked almost embarrassed with expectation but radiated good will, the kind of person who would move rapidly and with conviction to the front of any situation and, because of his hurry, miss significant details along the way but nevertheless have a firm opinion about what was going on. He shrugged off his trench coat—his baggy corduroy trousers were held up by braces—and drew his soft turtleneck up to his unshaven jaw. I took the bottle away from Sean's dignified little mouth, which went on sucking the air, and we all sat around the living room in a formal gathering, shy and awkward.

Jean-Paul began talking in rapid French about Armand, the person Niki wanted him to meet. But while he was talking, he kept his eyes on me as I spread out a towel, peeled off Sean's soaking wet nightie and held him up against my shoulder. Sean was such a thin old man, skin folded in little tucks under the armpits. Sophie started slapping at him with the flat of her hand.

"*Votre voyage en avion, il était bon,* it was okay?" Niki asked.

"*Mais oui.* It was fine. *Mais la nourriture!*" He made a face. "We couldn't eat that sausage. And the coffee—it was really terrible." He seemed pleased at finding the idiom.

"*Vous parlez anglais?*" I asked Loesic.

"*Oui. Je peux dire* the cow is in the meadow."

"That's it. That's all she can say," said Jean-Paul. "But she understands quite a bit."

She shrugged. She didn't care, we'd manage. She didn't tune out because I spoke a foreign language; instead, she slit her eyes above the smoke from the cigarette hanging on her lower lip, pushing her lips forward to watch my face as if she would get to know me from the way I talked rather than from the meaning of the words. She began putting the pieces of Sophie's toy town back in its net bag. Sean's fingernails were as long as a sorcerer's. Chew them off, the nurse had told me. I couldn't let go Loesic's eyes while I did it. Someone might have thought I was eating him, fingers first.

"*Café?*" Niki asked, heading for the kitchen, but she was sidetracked as they all began talking again rapidly in French. I couldn't concentrate the way Loesic did and felt stranded on the platform with the train disappearing down the track. A brief lull gave me a chance to reboard.

"Are you going to stay in London long?"

Loesic looked surprised. "*Peut-être.*"

"We don't have much room, but you're welcome to stay here."

Niki was becoming impatient and kept looking at her watch. "Look, I told Armand I'd bring you over as soon as you arrived. We have to take the tube. It's like the Metro, only cleaner."

Loesic shook her head. "*Nous sommes fatigués, Niki.*"

She pulled a tapestry bag with wooden handles out of her travel case, took out some balls of cotton thread, slowly put on her glasses and began to chain crochet stitches on a thick hook, alternating pale green and pink scallops, changing over to white once she'd made an edge. She'd taken in all the information she could for the moment, so she stopped watching and listening and focussed instead on her crocheting. She looked as if she would never move again.

At dusk the streetlights came on, old-fashioned lantern ones on cement poles with a blue glow that looked as if they should have someone in a raincoat singing underneath them. Occasionally Loesic glanced up as if to register the change in light from the dull opaque of the overcast sky to navy blue as the sky darkened. Sean's hand curled around my finger and the tiny perforations of skin around his fingers seemed punched from cardboard. I separated his fingers to get a better look. I'd asked about it in the hospital and the nurse had said the bits would fall off eventually, like cradle cap.

"*Le peau ici. Elle tombera . . . plus tard.*" I touched the tiny bits. "*Vous comprenez?*"

She looked over for a moment and smiled down at him. "*Oui. Vous n'êtes pas anglaise, Kathleen?*"

"*Non. Je suis canadienne. De la côte du Pacifique.*"

"*Ah.*"

So, I thought, dinner. "This beef you brought looks great. I think we should marinate it."

"*Oui.*"

I found a tablecloth. Passing the bread and wine, Jean-Paul alternated between being guarded when he thought no one was looking at him and dazzling us with bonhomie when we were. Sophie dressed for dinner in her red satin Chinese lounging pyjamas and spooned up mashed potatoes and applesauce.

I gave them the living room bed and moved a cot into the bedroom. Sean lay in the cradle facing one way at one end of the room, and Sophie lay in her crib facing the other. In the night I felt Loesic wake up and stare at the ceiling. Trust grows roots underground. My new friends slept there. That mattered.

Sophie was the first one awake the next morning and sat happily in a pool of sunlight playing with a toy skills set mounted on her bed, twirling the plastic telephone dial, zapping the levers, pushing the coloured beads up and down the rungs. Her fringe of blonde hair hung in her eyes. She squished a mess in her diaper so I got up, stripped her and washed her down. She ran around with no pants on as I sloshed her diaper up and down in the toilet.

Loesic had gotten up and gone into the kitchen to make coffee. I found her taking the percolator apart: the basket, stem and outside pot lay lined up on the kitchen counter. She shrugged, put the kettle on, lit a cigarette, sat on a stool and stared at the various components. I was trying to get Sophie to hold still so I could snap up her pants, but she squirmed out of my arms. Not letting me do up the snap was the game that morning and her pants kept falling down on one side. Then Sean woke up and the kettle started boiling all at once.

"Oh, wait a minute. You start with cold water, *de l'eau froide*. You don't need the kettle." With Sean in one arm, I filled the basket container with coffee and snapped on the lid. Sophie dragged her satin pyjamas over to Loesic, climbed back up on the round table by the window in the living room and dumped the pieces of the toy town all over the place mats. Jean-Paul's travel brochures from last night were spread out on the table and she was about to water them with her orange juice. He leapt out of bed.

"Oh, hey, Sophie," he laughed. "You don't like the galleries? What's the matter with you? The art critic here, Sophie." He began leafing through the brochures. "*Bien*, today we're going to see the Tower of London, the National Gallery, the Tate."

But they didn't. They didn't go anywhere. I was drawn to the heat in Jean-Paul, to the effort he had to make to take his eyes away from the cradle. His long flat cheeks pushed thin folds of skin up in the corners of his eyes. He said they hoped to see the paintings of Francis Bacon while they were in London.

Loesic asked me where I kept the vacuum cleaner but I didn't have one, so she did her best with the broom. She played with Sophie at sweeping a tiny bit of floor in the kitchen, and she found a grass skirt in Sophie's toy box and made a miniature one for Sophie's doll. Jean-Paul got some work out of his briefcase and settled down at the table. Loesic grew restless, as if she felt caged in the small apartment, and began prowling around. She seemed to be the kind of person who would instantly step outside in a new place to find out what was growing there.

"*Où est Niki?*" She hadn't come home the night before. She often didn't, I told Loesic, so we shouldn't worry. About eleven, she searched out a net bag behind the fridge, picked up her purse. "*Je vais faire les courses.*"

"Do you want me to come with you?"

"*Non.*"

"*Mais, Jean-Paul.* She doesn't know the stores, *les magasins. Voulez-vous accompagner votre femme?* Or . . ."

"Don't worry, Kathleen. *C'est bien.* It's okay."

Once she'd gone, I put the children down for their morning naps and headed for the studio—checking my watch. Because I didn't have to deal with the shopping I'd get maybe half an hour; I left Jean-Paul with the cold toast, the maps and the tourist brochures.

Never thought of trees as marching. You can't have trunks bending at the knee. Why not? So many, and then the hay. The hay Sean's lying in. Painting the castle in the rain forest. Build it there. A faint lift in the darkness. Sketches for the series in soft charcoals and greys, except for a mediaeval head of a woman in a wimple mounted on the last page. Each page had a hole. When you turned the pages, the face would stay in place staring through at the reader hard and glazed. I'd have to pad it somehow. Perhaps fabric like a pin cushion, or that kind of cracked leather. I wanted those cracks in the fabric like an old master's painting where the face is held together in a shattered mirror and a gust of wind would crack it into shards.

Across the channel, the night train whistled and the rain dripped, again the drip, the slip-crack ease of the top log giving way as the tide rose under the cottage. Another cardboard cutout of a castle when you turned the next page. *Morning dew beads the grass. The back is always in shadow.* The father could go off to face his spirits, alone. He would lie face down in the sand by the North Sea. Crash off through the forest to hunt. Dusky shadows everywhere. Lots of smoke through the smoke hole. I lifted up his hair and blew gently down his neck. The only way to stop the pain and hurt was to pretend I was his mother. The rites and complications of birth and labour frightened him, so Loesic would hold me instead over a birth pit lined in cedar. Think how I'd feel if you told me Sophie wasn't my daughter. Sophie wanted to be on a boat with a cargo of spices and silks heading for China. No, she didn't. Maybe for her sake Andrew would come back with food for the winter, regret his hasty decision, and slowly the lines of the family would reweave—including Jean-Paul and Loesic. Everyone could sleep apart, but not too far apart, all of us wrapped in our bear and deer skins on wooden platforms, and we would open our eyes not knowing if anyone else was awake and watch the fire.

Niki returned in the afternoon and Jean-Paul left with her to help her talk to the person who might have known her father in the war. Loesic read to Sophie while I shelled peas and baked a piece of mullet with dill for dinner. Maybe they could stay. We could get a bigger place. I loved having them there, the feeling of things being manageable because we were together. I didn't suppose Jean-Paul's business was the kind you could move. What if Andrew did come back? Then what? I'm making it all up, what I think about them, the way I see them. No, you're not. They're good solid people and they're not pretending. So he comes back? What if he rejects Sean? Then how will I keep track of it all? "Well, if it's too much for you,

Sophie can live with me. Your Honour, by her own admission my wife was unfaithful and admits to . . ." No. Sophie's completely tied up with me. Sean's only bonded to me by a few days. And I've been holding back from him. Does he feel that? Of course he feels that. It's no good. "Your Honour, there's every reason to believe . . . the paternity is in question, so how could I possibly be expected to . . .?" We'll go back to Spain. Then what? How would we live?

Plan B. I could get a full-time job and pay a sitter— which would leave barely enough money to get by and the kids wouldn't have me at home. If they only had one parent, they'd need more of me, not less.

Miserable options. I couldn't go home, not after I had gone home pregnant with Sophie after being deserted, not after everybody had told me not to go back.

"Ça va, Kathleen?" Loesic was looking up at me; she would tell me later, much later, that she took one look at me and knew I was feeling that I could manage one baby on my own but didn't think I could do a good job with two.

"I'm worried. I love Andrew, *mon mari. Sophie à besoin de son père.* I want him to come back. *Je suis très triste.*"

She sat on the stool, keeping her eyes down, then looked directly at me. We looked at each other a long time, both of us searching, questioning.

"*Mais il n'est pas le père, n'est-ce pas?*"

"Niki doesn't think so. *Je ne suis pas certaine.* He says he's not, which means he's not going to father him, so it comes to the same thing." I implied that Andrew wanted to be with me and Sophie (which I didn't believe) because I wanted him to be with us so badly.

She nodded as if she understood and spread out some

pictures of their country place, Bouchauds; it was lovely with the wall along the river and the long grass in front of the house. "*C'est beau. C'est très beau.*"

"Do you spend much time there?"

"As much as we can," she said, and then she looked up at me with her starving eyes.

That night I woke up crying with a cold. Loesic was up before me, dragging the enamel pot onto the gas ring. She made Sean's bottle and brought it to me, then she and Jean-Paul stayed up watching television and playing cards in the living room. By then he wasn't even bothering to put his papers back in his briefcase and had taken over the big table for his work, which we cleared away only at mealtimes. I didn't care. I was avoiding everything by pretending that they were staying. A car across the street smashed up against the wall. Later that night, for the second feeding, I stuck my feet into my mules, gave Sean my knuckle to suck as I carried him up the hall so he wouldn't wake Sophie, and heated his bottle in a pan of water. I sat down and fed him with cement arms. My hair came floating up the hall. His eyes opened as he sucked— come on, sweetheart—I tucked the blanket around his thin legs and curved them into my waist. I must have fallen asleep, and Sean too, falling off the end of the nipple, which slid out and popped back up on the other side of his mouth, making him jump and waking us both up.

Then I felt Loesic's thick hand on my shoulder, heavy rings on three of her four fingers. More blue ovoids, some almost circles between the branches. Navy black cedars on the wall in front of me.

"If I could just get some sleep through one feeding. I'm no good without sleep." She nodded. It was obvious what

I was saying. Somewhere the snow was slanting down the long cedars, turning into rain. The blip blip of the rain from the eaves and the counterpoint tripping faster off the ivy as the pan slid from the gas ring.

The next feeding time she was sitting up in bed with Jean-Paul beside her, leaning against the pillows embroidered with small mirrors, fingering them to get a feel of the fabric. White flannel nightgown, hair in a braid. Knock, no answer, knock again. The time after that she put the bottle inside the door and called. A faint lift in the darkness.

Suddenly I had to get out of there. I took the elevator down to the street, still in my nightie and dressing gown, and walked up and down in front of the apartment, hugging my arms. When it came to babies I knew. I couldn't count on Andrew. He wasn't stable. Even if he did come back for Sophie, I knew I was on my own in this. I had made that decision when I left Vancouver, even if I didn't know it at the time. These were my children and I had to make the best decision for the three of us, the one that would hold up best whether Andrew came back or not. What if? What if what? What if I? If I did . . . do that, that way he'd be safe. Nothing could touch him. He'd be protected. We'd all be safe. *You hardly know them.* I know enough. I've seen and heard enough to know what they're like. They're here and I need them and they need me. Can you allow that that much is true? *Yes, I can.* You don't need to agonize, throw yourself all over the stage. *Yes, I do. What did you do with that baby you had while I was away? I ate him.* What about my parents? I can't do this to them. I'll tell them. *No, you won't.* If we were together, the Richters and me, between the three of us we could raise two well-loved and well-cared-for children. *Forget it, you're alone.* When I'm tired I blame everyone. Andrew and I could never get back together after this. *Crap. That's why you're doing it. Without Sean, maybe he'll come back.* I've made them up, they're not really here. My parents will look at me and say nothing. They'll think I'm smiling too hard.

I went back up to the kitchen and found Loesic picking up the bottle, holding it out at arm's length. She squeezed a drop on her arm before she gave it to me—I was smelling her—as she passed Sean's cradle. She put down her finger and he grabbed it. But she didn't pick him up. He needed picking up right then and we both knew it. We stood staring at each other, his need engorging my breasts, blood I guessed, and I held back for that extra second. Suddenly I had a vision of the three of them in a meadow where for a moment there was just light as he flipped out of the cradle and into their arms and they threw him into the air. Not far, just up with the joy of it, in the air. They were outside in a meadow with the smell of newly cut grass. I stepped back from the hoop of fire. It was just once but it was there, a wheel of light and very very fast. I caught my breath because they were all three flipping backwards one after the other like tumblers on a gym mat. But really she hadn't touched him. Instead, we were arcing in graceless circles around each other. She went a long way out of her way to get past me in the hall, and I arrived late, awkwardly anesthetizing Sean from the moment of his need. This was no good, blindly going the long way around when the person I needed lived only a block away and I didn't know it until I was amazed to find myself back in my own neighbourhood. I lay down and tried to sleep again but woke up an hour later. The apartment felt like a doll house with the front wall removed exposing the partitions between the rooms. Loesic turned in bed against Jean-Paul. I felt her drift off, then I drifted off, then I sat bolt upright an hour later trying to think where the baby was. I dreamt my arms were slipping from under him so slowly and hers were coming up under mine so gently he didn't notice the difference. *He'll notice the difference.* All the breathing in the house—we were all still breathing—the sky was getting lighter. Jean-Paul, Loesic, Sean, then Sophie. Then Jean-Paul, then Loesic, then Sean, then Sophie. Then Sophie, then Jean-Paul, then Loesic, then Sean. Then Sean.

In the morning I couldn't stop looking at her lap where she sat in the chair—it looked like a stone basin—and I was so far out in front of myself by then I didn't know how to stop. All I wanted was some sleep, but we were at breakfast with our boiled eggs and crumbs and no place mats. *I'm sorry, Sophie.* We were in the middle of breakfast but I got up, went over and picked up Sean where he was lying in his cradle. Then came that split-second decision and I started to walk across the carpet with him on the flats of my hands *I'm sorry, Sean*—oh my god—the carpet was blue and my hands were cold—and when I looked up to see how far I had to go—I felt I might lose my balance— Loesic sat there looking at me calmly, as if wondering why it was taking me so long to get there. I either had to get him there or not. Suddenly I was in front of her laying him in her lap. Jean-Paul leapt up to stand beside her. The minute Sean was in her lap, Loesic took off her glasses, twisted her hair close to her neck, stuck a hairpin through it so she could sink her chin further into her shoulder. I wanted to be sitting on the floor with my head on her thigh and her hand on my hair and I couldn't move away, so I stood there before her, at once hollow and comforted. The egg hardened on our plates. Crumbs all over the dark blue carpet, a mistake anyway, it showed everything. Loesic gave off a thick glow, wave after wave of relief and joy as if she'd been carrying Sean for months. In the hospital, they'd tied a tight strip of bandage around my breasts, pressing them flat and hard against me, fastening the bandage with a butterfly clip like you do for a sprain. The pressure of the binding was supposed to dry the milk, but as I stood facing Jean-Paul and Loesic, my milk started up again. The front of my dress flooded and I was ashamed to look down. Loesic and I continued staring at each other, unable to stop what was happening or the milk; Jean-Paul wrapped his large hands around the boy, lifting the package of bones and skin carefully from his wife's lap onto his own shoulder, letting the baby's tiny hands paw at the air.

I dabbed a napkin in the glass of water on the table, my chin on my chest, and tried to get at the stains on the front of my dress. Sean's head flopped on his neck.

"You've got to keep your hand there," I said weakly.

"Yes."

"He needs to be burped." Neither of us knew what the word was in the other's language so I mimed it, patting a hump of baby-shaped air on my own shoulder. Jean-Paul began patting at the baby's back with a stiff wrist.

"Like this?"

"A little slower." I looked up from where I was still dabbing at my dress.

"How will I know when he's done it?" He kept straining over his shoulder trying to see him.

"You'll hear him."

Maybe this was supposed to be the arrangement all along. Sophie scrambled into my lap and cheerfully put her hand inside my dress. Sean managed a clear and unequivocal burp for Jean-Paul. Loesic reached over and touched Sean's cheek with her knuckle.

"Will it ever be possible . . .? Please, will you try to help him understand that it's because of who you are, not that I . . . I didn't . . . put him up for adoption. I would never do that." Translate, Jean-Paul.

"*Faites-nous confiance*," said Loesic.

"What did she say?"

"She said trust us."

I looked at her and I did.

"I guess," said Jean-Paul the next day, "we'd better think about getting back to Paris."

I guessed they'd better. He was putting on his shoes and I was sitting on their bed thinking about how mothers must have felt when they sent their children overseas during the war. Somehow I was going to have to get through these arrangements but, relieved as I was at the way they were handling him, picturing the warmth he would be basking in, the light from their faces beaming down at him, another part of me was alarmed. What had I done with my parents' grandchild?

Suddenly Jean-Paul sat up straight. "*Mon Dieu*, what are we going to do about immigration? He's not on either of our passports."

"I've thought about that, Jean-Paul. I left the father's name blank on the birth certificate. What do you think, Loesic, *Est-ce que tu permettras à ton mari d'être le père de notre fils?*"

"*Absolument.*"

We decided she would take the babies to Hyde Park while Jean-Paul and I went to the registry office. It was easier seeing her with Sean and Sophie together. I wasn't just going to lose Sean, I was going to lose them as well.

"Let's go," I said. "Let's get it done."

We were standing by the door, getting ready to go, when Niki came in. She hadn't been around much, perhaps she'd been staying away deliberately, I didn't know, but earlier that morning I had heard Loesic on the phone to her. She came in, gay and congratulatory. *Bonjour.* Kiss kiss. Kiss kiss. Kiss kiss. It occurred to me that it's a form of stalling, all this kissing, getting used to the person before you actually had to make contact. Her buoyancy made me angry.

I went into the kitchen with my coat still on and dejectedly began to dry the dishes. Niki beamed in announcing how beautiful the baby was, as if he'd changed since I last looked at him. Or as if now that he was theirs, he was somehow also hers. I put away a plate and forced myself to calm down because I wasn't done yet. I realized that because he was now theirs, Niki was also more theirs. They were all going to have each other and I wasn't going to be part of the equation.

All this left me feeling more isolated than I'd ever felt in my life. It was what I'd helped to create and it was best for everyone that they had each other. Yet standing there drying the dishes made me think of the times my mother would go out of her way to foster the bonds between me and the friends I brought home by insisting that we get on with our plans for the evening and leave the dishes to her.

I put my hand on the counter to steady myself for a moment and then found myself again at the end of the hall facing the curtained cupboard of empty coats and jackets.

"*Tu es certaine, Kathleen?*"

"*Oui*, Loesic, I am." I wasn't but I said I was.

Jean-Paul and I caught a taxi on Queensway. I leaned forward to tell the driver to take us to the Paddington registry office and, when I sat back, Jean-Paul was suddenly a handsome man in a trench coat. He looked at me perhaps thinking the same sort of thing, but I made myself turn away; if he was going to be the father of my child, I couldn't let there be any innuendo between us. I thought about my father and how, if he were here, he would be trying to turn the situation around as quickly as possible. As a child, when I was upset about something he thought I shouldn't be upset about, he'd tell me to stop crying or in one minute flat he'd give me something to really cry about. I was afraid of his anger but I loved and respected him. I looked at Jean-Paul again, thought about Loesic sitting under a tree with the babies and knew in my heart Sean would be happier with them than anybody and I had to stay with that.

"Paddington?" he said. "Like the little *nounours*, what is it, bear? In a blue jacket? *Sans pantalon?*"

"That's the one."

We could have been friends, these people and I.

At the registry office we sat sedately on hard-backed chairs in a room lined with cardboard boxes of manila files. The clerk sitting behind the desk wore plastic sleeve cuffs so as not to soil the sleeves of her blouse. I crossed my legs and uncrossed them and crossed them the other way, took my identification out of my purse and handed it across the desk.

"You have a birth certificate here I filed a week ago when my son was born. We're here to register the father's name on the certificate. Mr. Richter would like to make a formal entry, to be formally entered on the certificate."

"Yes, of course, M . . . I'm sorry."

"Richter. Jean-Paul Richter."

"You're the father of this child?"

"I'm the father of this child."

Jean-Paul leaned forward to watch her get down the file box. As she presented him with the document, holding it in both hands, and he took his fountain pen to sign his name, his face was so absorbed it occurred to me it was just as well this wasn't the same clerk who came by my bed in the hospital: she would have realized that this man would not be willingly away from his son longer than it took to get a meal.

"There you are. Two copies. One for the mother and one for the father." We stood out on the sidewalk, blinking in the glare.

"What do we do now?" he said.

"We go to the passport office."

At the passport office we showed them the birth certificate and explained that we needed a passport so the baby could go to France with his father. They told us we needed a picture so we went home and took Sean to have his photograph taken. Jean-Paul went into detail with Loesic about the clerk's plastic sleeve cuffs, demonstrating their shape on his wrists and shaking his head. At the photographer's, Jean-Paul wrapped Sean in a receiving blanket the way I showed him and held him up to the camera with both hands.

The next morning they got ready to leave. We had all the baby equipment to pack: extra formula, bottles, sheets and blankets. Sophie and I went down to the street to say good-bye to them. As they opened the doors and put their bags in the front of the taxi, I folded up the stroller and put it in the trunk. Then Loesic turned around with her arms open and asked us to come to see them in Paris as soon as we felt ready. I had no idea when or if I'd be able to handle that but I nodded and hugged her back. Jean-Paul and I embraced as he stood up from where he sat on the back seat. When they drove away, Loesic turned to wave through the back window like a departing bride.

Sophie and I went back upstairs. I closed the door and leaned against it. Every morning they'd been there, Loesic had leaned her elbows on the table, taken an orange from the bowl and peeled it in a spiral with a paring knife. She tucked the top into a hard bud and twisted the rind around her hand, easing it down into a rose. Then she slid her palm out so the rose lay on the table. She'd left five of them lined up on the window ledge. I sat on their bed and stared at my feet. I fed Sophie her flakes of cardboard muesli. Then I wrote to my parents and broke their hearts.

2

So, Mom, how's it going?" Sophie came back with the milk.

Gresco's house was on a busy street and the trucks lunged past, gearing down to the corner. Dark clouds closed in back of her and the rain smeared the grey-brown buildings and the streets, but she was bright coming down the lane where bits of grass poked through the asphalt. I waited for her on the back porch.

"Fine. Do you want some help?"

She shouldered open the screen door and let me in first, then took a brick of ice cream from the fridge. The fridge door dangled on one hinge. She scooped a knifeful from the carton into the blender and whirred it.

"Want some of this smoothie, Mom?"

"Oh, thanks, Sophie. That'd be nice." She poured the thick foaming drinks into beer glasses, put one down in front of me.

"You have to go pick up Luke or what?"

"No, he's on his bike."

The bread board was familiar, a wooden pig outlined in black that I had bought at a garage sale. I'd been wondering what had happened to it. The cat dish smelled and the wastebasket was full of ashes and cigarette butts. The television upstairs was hawking fertilizer.

Gresco came down the stairs, legs splayed, one pant leg made from an old American flag and the other from a Union Jack. He was tall with a narrow lean face and, as Sophie put it, always wore the worst clothes he could find on purpose. His pants were at least a size too small and the sleeves of his shirt came halfway up his forearms. He moved all the debris down to one end of the table, grabbed a chrome chair and sat on it backwards. He heaped a spoonful of brown powder into a striped mug, then helped himself to the white powder decanted into an upside-down hubcap.

"I got some milk," said Sophie.

"I like this poison better. Hey, how are you, Sophie's mom?"

"Pretty good, Gresco. How's the music business?"

"Can't complain." He turned to Sophie. "Are you going to work today, Sophie Sophie?"

Sophie worked part-time at a shop called Angel, a poster and fabric paint store over by the library. She was tired of it but was determined to finish her degree and needed the money. She sat down on a packing case and smeared her toast with veggie butter.

"I'm glad you came over this morning, Mom, because I was going to call you anyway. The thing is, Gresco's band has to go to L.A. next week and there's a problem getting them across the border. If they go down together, they'll know they're going down to work and they're already on the computer at both border crossings, the one at Blaine and the other one."

"Really?"

"Yeah, so the thing is, they have to go down one at a time and we were thinking that if Gresco put his baseball hat on backwards and, like, really slouched down in the seat and you drove him, he could pass as your son." My son? My son left for Paris waving his tiny hand like a maple leaf.

"So, Mom, will you do it?"

Loesic ripped Sean off my chest like ripping off adhesive. *She did not.*

"Sure be nice if you'd drive me down there, Sophie's mom."

"Sure, Gresco, no problem." As I got up to go, he picked up the invitation.

"This yours?" He started to hand it to me.

"No, it's Sophie's."

"No, Mom, you take it. You're the one. Really."

Sophie and I got in the car and drove slowly downtown. Just below the viaduct, the Expo dome was going up, and outsized cranes were bent over opposite sides of the carapace like pincers. Sophie looked at me sideways. "Do you know what Loesic told me when I was over there, Mom?"

"No, what did Loesic tell you when you were over there, Sophie?"

"She told me she wanted to present Sean back to you. She said you'd given him to her, and now that he's grown up, she wants to present him back to you."

Sophie had taken on too much of the burden in this, I

knew that; she was the only one in the family who'd met him. I felt I certainly should go if only to get her off the hook, but I wasn't sure that was a sufficient reason. Maybe it was.

Sophie was eight years old when I first told her about her brother who had been adopted and had gone to live in France. She was in the bath. I'd shampooed her hair straight up on top of her head in a stiff peak like a meringue.

"There you are, you're Miss Dill Pickle." It was a game my mother had played with me. She'd learned it from her mother who had played it with her.

"Yes, it's funny. No, you can't go to school like that. Put this facecloth over your eyes. We have to rinse it out. Come on, Sophie, do what I say."

"The soap hurts."

"Remember we were at the beach today, and we saw that barnacle, the one that looked like a turret?"

"No."

For years I had been telling her a story about a miniature family who lived on the beach and wore pointed shoes and bluebell hats. *In those days, Sophie, there was hardly any difference between fairies and other people. Everyone was the same size. The men were tall enough to sleep comfortably under large mushrooms, and the women, if they didn't mind the swaying, soft enough to settle comfortably into the larger variety of blowsy rose . . .*

She clenched her teeth and refused to tip her head back: instead, stood up to be rinsed. Streaks of soapy water slid down her shiny chest and legs.

"That's enough. No more rinses. The soap's all out."

"One more."

I wrapped a towel around her. She sat down hard on the edge of the bathtub and stared at the floor.

"I want a real brother or sister, not any more fairies."

I wiped away the ring. "Do you, Sophie?"

"Yes, I do."

I stood up and stared at the bathtub, and then went to the living room and took a rosewood box from a high shelf. About a year after they'd left London, the Richters sold Bouchauds and bought a ruin of an old castle they'd been looking at for years. They sent me pictures. It was an architectural disaster, more of a ruin than a dwelling. The whole roof had fallen into the middle so the walls around the top resembled the rim of a crater. They'd said the money they got from selling Bouchauds would only be enough to pay for fixing the roof.

They'd had the photographs made into postcards. The first card, in black and white, showed large chunks of rock falling off the top of the castle. I shuffled it to the bottom of the pile. By the time the second card arrived years later, the structure was dark and elegant with violet shadows illuminated by spotlights. Next came a snapshot of Sean in a black wool sweater running through an arrangement of rocks that looked like Stonehenge. In another, he was holding on to the wrought iron railing of the narrow balcony outside their apartment in Paris and had turned his face up to the first few flakes of snow, about to catch them on his tongue. In another picture, taken on Valentine's Day, he wore a terry-cloth jumpsuit and was tucked into a bentwood rocking chair. Jean-Paul and Loesic stood on guard on either side of him, holding tall sunflower stalks like lances. The three of them were framed in a heart cut from red construction paper. I used to look at these pictures for hours, trying to fill in the details and imagine what he did in the days that went by between the snapshots. I never forgot, never forgot seeing them drive away and going back upstairs, never forgot the look of him in her arms, never stopped feeling guilty.

I went out to the porch and stared into the ridge of the north shore mountains. Behind the first range, more mountains and valleys and lakes and plains all the way to the north pole. Hardly any people in there. Somewhere, beside a lake, a deer would look up from drinking if you guessed its name correctly.

When I turned around, Sophie was right behind me, still wrapped in the towel, looking at me accusingly.

"This is going to be a surprise to you, Sophie, but because of something that happened a long time ago, you do have a brother. He's a year younger than you and his name is Sean."

"Can I go play with him?"

"Someday, but he lives in France and we'd have to go on a plane. This is his picture."

She took the one of him romping through the stones and looked at it critically. "He's too little. He's too little for me to play with."

"That was a few years ago. He's older now."

"Oh."

"I was alone when he was born. Your dad had . . . to be away."

Once upon a time there was a man and a woman who longed for a child. They looked everywhere. Down into the mouths of ladyslippers . . .

How many times had we read *Tom Thumb* before I told her the real story? Once she heard the real story, she wanted it over and over again.

A month after they'd left London, I took Loesic up on her invitation and went to Paris. Their flat was on the top floor of an apartment building in the area just below Pigalle. There were five flights of stairs. No elevator. How did she do it with a pram? She answered the door, slid the fruit I'd brought onto the hall table without looking at it and reached out her arms for Sophie.

There was a large room with a high-ceilinged office-studio for Jean-Paul, who stood behind his wife with his arms stretched out, waving them up and down as if he were making an angel in the snow. He looked anxious. "Have you come to take the baby?"

Loesic put her solid hand on his arm. "Shush, of course she hasn't. Come and see him."

She led me into a hushed room, the door slightly open onto a narrow balcony with wrought iron railings. The curtains were pale and the air was amber. The centrepiece of the room was a high-standing bentwood cradle lined with blue gingham and matching pillows. It had side padding and a canopy draped from a circular stand over the bed. Above it hung a mobile of carved wooden puppets. Sean lay there, sleeping like cream in a wide smooth calm with blue shadows on his eyelids; the aura of love and care around him was palpable. I put my arms around Loesic and we both held on tight for a few minutes.

I stepped up closer as we tiptoed in on the thick carpet.

The room was full of clean stuffed toys. He had the same broad forehead as Sophie, Andrew's wide space between his eyes, Andrew's skin, Andrew's ironic smile even as he slept.

"*Il est beau, hein?*" My face drained. She couldn't know what I was thinking.

"He sure is." She held me firmly in her look and told me that she had to go out shopping. I knew she knew that I would not undo what I had done. Even so, my chest grew small hooks like burrs, and as I sat formally in their living room with Sophie on my knee, I prayed that he wouldn't wake up.

The next day we drove to Bouchauds. We arrived to find the wattled brown house waiting for us along the river. Inside the house I wandered around touching everything, the tablecloth, the dishes, the chairs. Jean-Paul explained all the features as if I were a prospective buyer. That evening, he took a candle and led me through a trail in the woods until we came to a small tower where Sophie and I would sleep. It was strange and magical out there in that baroque bed with a tapestry hanging on a whitewashed wall. In the morning, we sipped bowls of milky coffee and ate thick toasted bread. Friends called and came by. I didn't know if they knew who I was or not. Sophie, in the white crocheted dress trimmed with green and pink scallops that Loesic had sent to London, climbed in and out of Sean's cocooned hammock tied between two wildly blossoming cherry trees. She was passed from lap to lap. Gaiety seemed to be an everyday affair, *les fêtes quotidiennes*. No one minded me, and the language barrier provided protection. I couldn't pick up complications or innuendos. When the chocolate boiled over on the stove, Loesic jumped up to get it and handed Sean to me without thinking.

In the afternoon, Jean-Paul poled us out on the river in a punt and Loesic and I held our babies on our laps like any two mothers. The water shone. Jean-Paul sat down to paddle rather than pole through some thick algae. "I'm in a canoe," he said. "Like that other father, the Blackfoot."

The colours shivered fiercely as in a Seurat. The sun expanded to white heat and I slit my eyes, wishing I had my sunglasses. I said, "There's not even an outside chance he's the father. Not now."

But they didn't seem to hear me. Jean-Paul just continued paddling and smiling as if there was nothing wrong.

Back in Paris we arranged to sign the adoption papers. Jean-Paul ushered me into his lawyer's office and went around behind the desk to help sort out the documents. The lawyer translated the part about the transfer of parental rights.

"That sounds fine," I said. "But I want to add something." Jean-Paul's expression turned to one of alarm.

"I want a clause added stating the Richters are to keep in touch with me by mail so that I know how Sean is getting on, and that I be notified at once if anything should happen to them."

I explained to the lawyer and Jean-Paul that I wouldn't come and take Sean away in the event of an emergency since his people and language—his *patrimoine*, as the French would say—would be here, but I would come. That was our agreement. That was our understanding.

The next day in the hall when Sophie and I were leaving, we all stood in a circle of hugs and murmured that we would see each other soon, maybe in Spain. The children could swim in the turquoise sea. Loesic said that I would know the right time to come back, that I must trust myself to know. She said she would make it all right for him about having two mothers. I longed for these days to continue when we were all together, but I couldn't put Sean in the position of looking back and forth between the two of us. And I couldn't ask the Richters to do it any other way but with the full protection of a formal agreement. It wouldn't be right.

I didn't see him again for eighteen years.

Sophie and I returned to London and I threw myself into my work. She liked to sit at her small table with her crayons and paints while I was working, then we'd take a break and go to the park. I ate out of the frying pan standing up at the sink. I found more part-time work in the schools and she went to a sitter three afternoons a week. That left marginal profit, but we managed. We were okay. Under the circumstances, I thought okay was a lot.

I was working on a series of lifeboat paintings, the boats broken in half, stranded on banks of sea grass. The idea had come to me one night when the Richters had still been with us and I had pulled the cradle up the hall, like a lifeboat when the tide was coming up, so when the baby woke up he wouldn't wake Sophie. One day I had finished work on one of the paintings and was about to wash the kitchen floor. I had just run water into the sink and stuck in the mop when I heard a key in the lock. The door opened and Andrew stood there in his duffle coat. He put down his suitcase. Sophie had started to walk at last, not just toddle, and she came running out of her room to climb into the chair he always made by crouching down and curving his arms, tightening her arms around his neck and her legs around his chest so that he stood up again with her latched onto him. Despite the circumstances, there was a moment of relief: The weight's off. Daddy's home.

I moved the garbage bin and the stool out of the kitchen as she pulled him into her room and made a big point of closing the door. In the bathroom I picked up everything—the soap powder, sponges and rack dryer—threw them in the bathtub and desperately started to wash the floor, pretending that I hadn't seen him, he hadn't really come, insulating myself until I could take it, making my body go on with its usual movements. When I finished, I went into Sophie's room and told them both it was time for Sophie's nap. Once I got her hushed we went back out.

"So how'd it go in Newcastle?"

"Fine."

"Where are you going to stay?"

"Here."

"No."

"It's my house too. Why don't you leave?"

"Pardon?"

"You've made some mess of it, though."

"Don't, she's . . . Did you bring any money?" I started whispering.

"Some, why?"

"We need some."

"Uh-huh."

I began to clean some paint brushes, gave up and turned back to him.

"Aren't you even going to ask me about the baby?"

"I heard about that."

"Oh, I see. So you understand then."

"Why? He's not mine. I think I have more right to stay here than you do. "

"Well, no, you don't, actually. Andrew, let's not fight, let's just see if we can work something out for her sake. Please."

In the next few days, I tried to keep doing what I would have been doing anyway, knowing something would have to give even if I didn't force the issue, because what had happened was irrevocable. If not knowing whether Sean was his was really the reason Andrew had left—as he said; deep down I doubted it—I had to give him the option of making good his declaration. It was only fair to Sophie and it was one reason I had made the decision I did. I didn't actually think of it in terms of calling his bluff, but that's what I was doing.

By now I knew there'd been a mistake. Should I have told them all to go away and waited to see if Andrew came back? Maybe. I didn't know. I did know for certain after seeing him in Paris that Sean was Andrew's baby. But I couldn't say so while the Richters were in such a delicate position, solidifying their family. I had to protect them. It was done. There was no going back. Every time I looked at Andrew, I thought about Sean lying in that bentwood cradle. It was just awful. I found it impossible to talk because the unspoken truth lay under everything. It was like a bomb ready to explode and blow the appearance of normal life sky high. But normal life had to be maintained to protect Sean and the Richters.

The air between us was like shards of broken glass. I couldn't say anything and I couldn't not say anything. It was as if I had woken up with a nightmare that all this had happened but, when I got up to get a drink of water, the Richters were actually sitting in the bathroom. Not only did Andrew not know who they were, he pretended he didn't see them. With him there, all I could think about was how the baby was getting on, whereas I'd been managing to forget about him for perhaps an hour or so a day when Sophie and I were alone. Having Andrew back made it worse. The hole in our family gaped at me.

Neither of us talked much. We were as numb as if we had been anesthetized. We had stumbled into this situation on our own, and neither incompetence nor inexperience was an excuse. Andrew didn't seem the least bit touched by the gesture I'd made in letting the Richters adopt Sean, didn't even seem to be thinking about whether I'd done it for the good of the family or not. His way was not to talk about it at all. He pretended—and I tried to pretend—that the people from the hospital, the Richters, the baby, were not physically with us. But they were, and the only way we could be in the apartment together was to pretend to be blind. One day a crack opened in the kitchen linoleum. It gaped wider every day. I hid money in it.

Seeing Sophie with her dad was the only compensation, and it was what kept me there. He was tender with her, and sweet, but he started to stay away from the flat more and more. It was no surprise to any of our friends when he moved in with a girl friend of mine. That hurt for a long time, and I ached for Sophie. Every time I thought she might be needing her father, I tried to turn up my love a notch to make up for it, but it wasn't the same.

Andrew would show up again years later when we were living in New York. He called and came by, fell into my arms at the door as if he'd been leaning against it for a long time. He smelled the same, wet and tender. By that time, I had remarried and Luke had been born. Andrew was very nice to Luke. He had brought Sophie a doll, a Sasha doll, and insisted on showing it to me before we went down the hall. He had made a point of getting one with blonde hair, so it wouldn't be too much like her—we were both dark—and when Sophie looked up at him from under her blonde bangs, he didn't know what to say. He looked depressed and said he'd thought that the blonde hair she had had when she was little was baby hair, if I knew what he meant.

In all the years of thinking about Sean and looking at the pictures Loesic and Jean-Paul sent, it had never seemed like the time to go. I had convinced myself that our connection would transcend distance and nationality. We would commune across continents and oceans if need be. We would pull words out of the air. But I knew it was wishful thinking, all that postpartum logic. That young woman who was me back in the sixties running around Europe changing costumes was almost a stranger now, but even she had known you couldn't carve your life into little segments and imagine that they didn't affect one another. You collapsed that soufflé, told that person off, had that child, and there was no going back.

When Sophie was eighteen and beginning to think about travelling, it had occurred to me that one of the advantages of these extended families—and god knew there were lots of disadvantages—would be that, at this fledgling age, she would have more than one home base where she could safely touch down. She had a stepfather and his family in New York now as well. If Loesic were a good mother—and I counted on her to be a good mother—might she feel as I did, that she would want Sean to be aware of possible resources away from home? In that case, my visit would be appropriate. *Je veux être une ressource dans ta vie?*

There might never be a better occasion. Perhaps it would be easier for him to meet me in a ritualized situation with all his friends and family around him, instead of uprooting himself later on and coming to the door where we'd all sit down too naked in the living room. And this way he would know that I had come just to be at his party. So? After all, he knew—I resisted saying it—that I had given him up, let him go. If I had this to do over again, I would write a letter addressed to Sean, telling him in my own words why I had decided to do what I did and my feelings and hopes for him and his life. I'd been told that it helps for the adoptive parents to have something concrete to show the child when they tell him about his natural parents. Whoever he was, he had every right to feel angry and cheated, and my appearing would put him in a position where he would be expected to dilute his feelings. Right? Of course Sophie wanted me to go. What if he didn't even want to talk to me? But at least I'd know who he was when I thought about him.

In French, *invitation* is feminine, and if I were Loesic and she were me—I am Loesic, she is me. *That's a lie, a mask to deny your sense of guilt and loss.*

Maybe there was an outside chance that he'd attached the note to the invitation and sent it to my place instead of Sophie's because he wanted to ask me directly but was afraid I'd say no. But that didn't wash. The invitation was to Sophie, not me, and I knew it.

In the following week, I wrote different versions of the same letter to Sean and Loesic and Jean-Paul, crumpled them up and threw them out. I couldn't concentrate. I tried to put it out of my mind and go about all the normal things, but the question kept coming back to me like one of those balloon dolls with flat feet you knock down only to have it snap right back up.

One morning I forgot and put the raisins in the granola before putting the pan in the oven. They dried out and Luke carefully picked them out, saying oh, well, Mom, the road to perfection is long and difficult. Good-bye, Mom. So long, Luke. Have a good day at school. *Au revoir, Maman. À demain, Sean.*

Chers Jean-Paul et Loesic, I have in front of me your enticing invitation. *J'ai devant moi votre invitation si attrayante.* Sophie can't come. *Elle vous envoie ses regrets et ses bons baisers.* An evening of gods and goddesses at Pruniers under the full moon will be unforgettable. *Une soirée de dieux et déesses à Pruniers pendant la pleine lune sera mémorable à n'en point douter.* The fairies and woodspeople appear to be travelling to a *fête.* Do you remember the day you washed my face in lilacs?

I went out to the backyard and chopped my way through half a cord of alder. I piled the pieces up in the crook of my arm and stacked them under the house. I tried to imagine what it would be like at the fête, how I would actually *offre lui les philtres, poudres, talismans et sortilèges* and extend him . . . *les voeux étincelants et goûtez avec lui les étranges douceurs.* Sparkling wishes. The bizarre softness of Pruniers.

You could almost say that I had made Andrew up, sitting on my bed back in first-year university, casting him in Alain-Fournier's *The Wanderer* and thinking of him as Byronic. Sneaking out in the middle of the night with my friend Mary in our nighties, giggling under the rhododendron bushes. It took me most of my twenties to get over Eustacia Vye, Hardy's dark lady on the moors. We would look at Andrew sitting dark and alone over his coffee—the cafeteria was in a basement with windows at ground level—and I would say things to Mary like, "Maybe his mother was a gypsy."

"Maybe she was."

No different, really, from the days when we had gone to the Saturday matinees and sat on the bus afterward pretending we were Loretta Young. No, not pretending. We *were* Loretta Young. Thinking about getting married in those days was just as much a part of the game. One day you would be Elizabeth Taylor in *Father of the Bride* and then you would be a woman. That would be what made the difference. It wouldn't be when you graduated from university or when you had a job. It would be when you went home, or wrote home, that you had a husband. That was when you became an adult.

I gave up trying to come to a decision and drove along 41st Avenue past the old Kerrisdale Theatre, where we'd endured boys blowing peas on the backs of our necks at Saturday matinees, and stopped in to visit my mother. She was in her garden at the bottom of the slope in the backyard looking over the river, alert and elegant in the gardening gloves Sophie had made for her at the shop. Roses painted on all the knuckles. My mother said they were too good for anything but cutting roses. She wanted me to see the poppies. There was lobelia and white carnation, and over there she'd cut back the orange blossom. I had trouble that day responding to her regular garden tour. For her part, she had to look away from me when I talked about anything other than Sophie and Luke.

When Sophie had gone to Paris to visit the Richters, Mother and I talked about it as if she were only going to study at L'Alliance Française. Where she was staying was taken care of; we didn't need to go into the details. But once, shortly after Dad died, when we were sitting in the living room, my mother had said quietly, looking at the fire, that she wanted to meet Sean before she died. She picked up the tongs I'd bought her as a present when I came back from England and put them down again.

"Come into the house, dear. Do you want a cup of tea?" I picked up the tools and put them in the tool barrel. Her neighbour had tied strips of fluorescent ribbon around the handles of the gardening tools to make them easier for her to find. It was a hot day and the only cool place was under the maple tree. We sat with our teacups in the yellow chairs on the patio so that we could enjoy her snapdragons, which were out in a good show. She wanted me to take the lounge chair and shifted it to a better angle on the indoor-outdoor carpet.

"Did you leave the cottage the way you found it?"

"Yes, I always do." The saucer clinked as I put down the cup. "I have to tell you, Mother. I've had some news about Sean. They're having a coming of age party for him, and—I know this will be difficult for you—but I thought I might go."

"Who is?"

"The Richters."

"How are you going to do that?"

I moved the teacup slightly. "I . . . I don't know. For some reason, I feel I should. I've never felt like this before. It would be a way to introduce myself and then we could invite him over here if it was all right with the Richters. I could send him a ticket. You said once . . ."

"Yes, I know I did." She got up abruptly and went into the kitchen, came back with more hot water and said kindly perhaps she shouldn't interfere with my instincts on this. The fact that she rose to the occasion of my announcement filled me with relief and gratitude.

"Yes, it's odd they should be so strong now when I've never felt I should go before."

She carefully retied the belt of her dress and patted it into place, pulled her TV tray closer, keeping the line of her mouth thin. She looked a little frail that morning and had been out early to perform a delicate grafting job on her Tropicana.

"But, really, I don't see how you can do this, dear. That invitation was to Sophie. It's their triumph, this party. He won't want to see you or hear about Sophie and Luke. You didn't give *them* away."

She's right. I have no idea what they're like or their world. Get your pawns on the right squares. I mustn't let need interfere with judgement. But Loesic said I'd know when to come.

"I'll help you with the money if you do decide to go. But you know I would have used it to help Sophie next year."

My hands were growing more like hers, stiffer in the knuckles. I leaned over to straighten the magazines into a neater pile on the side table. I could hear someone next door banging plants out of their flower pots with the back of a trowel.

"Anyway, what about Lucas?"

"Luke is going to camp next week and then to visit his dad."

"Oh, that's right." She sighed and pulled a few dead leaves from the lemon geranium in the pot beside the stairs. *I should have made a bigger fuss over the dahlias. I shouldn't start. Say "Good-bye, Mom, I'll call later." Say . . .*

"Back then, I thought that if the three of us . . . if I let Jean-Paul and Loesic in, we would have two well-cared-for children." *I shouldn't be saying this. She and Dad never gave anything less than their best.* "I don't mean that like it sounds."

"Why don't you just leave it like that? You don't want to take away from their night."

Is that what I'd be doing? She's underlining all my fears. This is one thing in my life I've done right and I don't want to make a mistake now. "Maybe you're right. I'll give it more thought."

She looked pleased as she walked me to the car.

I pulled away but parked again halfway down the hill, a couple of blocks farther on. Whenever I was at my mother's house I struggled with my feelings of being an extension of her. I knew that, smiled wryly to myself and started the car again. I needed another opinion.

My second cousin, from Saskatchewan originally, lived in Vancouver's Point Grey area and had two daughters who were both adopted children. Her living room was crowded with a plaid sofa, card tables and the parts of her grandmother's dining room suite that didn't fit into the alcove. She wore glasses, had finger-permed hair and was married to my brother. After I told them what was up, she took out a picture of her father taken on the prairies on his wedding day. He had the same smile as Sean. My brother joined us, sitting on the edge of the matching plaid chair. He and I had never talked about Sean. The family had put my aberration down—with understandable bitterness—as a foible of my gypsy days in London, the sort of thing I'd be likely to get up to back then in my feather boas and capes in the Portobello Road. "I think you should go and I say this as the mother of two adopted children."

"But if it were you, wouldn't you feel . . .?"

"It's a bit different," she said gently. "You've been in touch all these years, and wasn't it because of a special understanding among the three of you?"

"Who told you that?"

"Your mother."

"Well, yes, but what would I go as?"

"You'll go as a friend of the family."

Suddenly I had to leave the room. I found myself in their backyard sitting on the bottom ledge of the wooden fence staring at the grass. Likely, if I went back in, we'd talk desperately about something else. Anything else. Instead, I leaned on the back porch railing and called up to them to say good-bye.

"This isn't easy," I added.

"No, but you'll figure it out."

I was glad at that point someone seemed to have faith in me.

Up in the attic in the north tower lies a woman with her head on a pillow and beside her on the pillow lies a tiny young man. Sean, she says. O'Seany O'Shay. You may be dreaming. Like as not we're all dreaming, but this wrapping we're bundled in, this night shift of wide white linen, is not all we intended it to be. I dreamt this a few nights before Sophie was born. I had given birth to a six-inch man who bowed and said his name was Sean.

The door banged, which told me Luke was home from school. He dragged himself up the stairs and into the kitchen, plunked down in a chair, dropped his baseball glove on the floor and reached down to pat the dog.

"Hi, honey."

Silence.

"What's wrong?"

"I hate myself."

"Why? Why do you say that?"

"We're going to do an operetta at school and I'm not going to sing or act. I have to dance."

"Maybe that won't be so bad."

"It'll be awful." He sat in his soccer shorts and loose T-shirt, sturdy thighs planted firmly on the chair, looking through the kitchen doorway to my bedroom where a canvas sack, make-up, a raincoat, a phrase book, a navy-blue cardigan, a couple of shirts and my seersucker skirt lay on my bed.

"What's all that?"

"It's my stuff."

"I know it's your stuff. What's happening?"

"You know that letter I had for Sophie?"

"Yeah."

"It's an invitation to a party they're having for Sean in France." He looked at the gear.

"So you're going?"

"I'm thinking about it. Sophie can't go and she wants me to go in her place. It wouldn't be until after you left for camp."

"You should go, Mom. It'd be nice for you. And Sean too."

He got up suddenly and went to his room, and I heard him slamming the lever on his pinball machine. I followed him and leaned against the doorway. "What kind of a dance is it they want you to do, anyway?"

"Some kind of folk dance."

"Oh." Luke was a kid who liked soccer, baseball and his dog. He stood half-leaning against the wall, tongue pushing out his cheek, the way he always did when he was concentrating.

"What would we do with the dog?"

"We'll have to think about that. You must be really looking forward to seeing your dad."

"I am." He looked up at me. "What would you do if you found out your dad was still alive?"

"Cry, I guess."

"Really."

The phone rang back in the hall. I went to answer it. A decal of a cartoon hippo was pasted on the circle on the phone where the number was supposed to be. Things Are Getting Worse, it said. Please Send Chocolate. I stood there peeling it off with my nail.

"Hi, Mom."

"Hi, Soph, what are you up to?" I stretched the phone

cord into the kitchen to check the zucchini loaf in the oven, moving the dog out of the way with my foot.

"Well, Mother, if you must know, Gresco came home with a horrible television set for a birthday present and I'm sitting on the bed watching it. I hate the hideous colour but at least I can see the excellent shade of the wine on this wine-tasting show."

"I didn't know you were interested in wine tasting."

"I'm not. I'm making a point about the colour, the colour of the TV."

"Ah, yes. I'm getting a bit slow in my old age."

"So I see. Well, the fellow here says it's meant to taste fruity. An unpretentious little wine. It's not meant to be flat on the tongue. Fruit cut with acidity. When you hold it up to the light, it should be pale, but not too pale. The cast should be gold with pale green highlights."

"Just a minute, Sophie." I covered the receiver and called back down the hall. "Luke, would you mind picking some lettuce for dinner?"

"Later."

"No, now."

"Oh, is he engrossed in a TV commercial again? 'Don't bug me, I'm watching this great ad.' The pain of it all . . ."

"Don't make fun of him."

"Right. Poor Luke."

"It's not easy for him."

"I'll say. Going to camp. Going wind-surfing."

"You went to Europe."

"And I raised most of my own fare. And paid some expenses."

"I know, Sophie," I said gently. Luke's dad spent money on him; Sophie's didn't. It wasn't easy for her.

"So are you going to go or what?"

"I honestly don't know if it's a good idea. I want to. I'd love to go, but I'm worried about intruding. Do you think I should?" She was the one who'd stayed with them, after all. But I immediately regretted asking the question, putting her in the role of the mother. That'd happened too often. One of the hazards of being alone.

"Yes, I do. Whenever it happens you're all going to be nervous."

I shoved the dog downstairs because Luke actually seemed to be on his way out to the garden. "I'd have to go a ways ahead of time. I don't know if I could get everything ready."

"But it's Sean's fête." Her silence was hard over the phone.

"Sophie, listen to me. I'd have to get a cheap night flight and then sit up on the Dover train and then that deadly ride into Paris at the crack of dawn and all those buses and metros. What's the station you leave from? Where do you go, anyway?"

"Poitiers. You go to Poitiers. I've got maps. You get the train from Gare d'Austerlitz to Poitiers and then Poitiers to the village."

"It sounds awful."

"Not really."

"Well, if I do go, I'm not going to take any baggage. I'm going to pack the same as I would for a hiking trip. I don't want to be lugging a suitcase across Paris . . ." I sensed her smiling.

"Fine, whatever."

Luke had changed his mind and come back upstairs, and he was stomping down the hall to the bathroom, dragging his hand along the wall. A ring around the house at kid level.

"Just in case you didn't know," he muttered. "My name isn't Luke any more. It's A. J. Springer."

"Have you got the darn lettuce yet, A. J.?"

"No, I'm going."

"Thin it, please, don't just pull out a whole bunch." I rumpled his hair as he went by on the way to the bathroom, but he pulled away from me. He left the door open so he could listen. I felt torn between the sense I had that no matter what he was saying he might feel insecure with the idea of me going so far away and Sophie's hopes. As usual, when I was responding to one of them, my sight lines to the other were blocked.

I grabbed a piece of paper. "Okay, so how do you say, 'anticipating a complicated trip'?"

"*Prévoyant. Prévoyant un voyage compliqué.*"

" 'By foot if I have to.' No, I'll take that out. It's too dramatic."

"No, leave it in. He'll like it."

"*Prévoyant un voyage compliqué*, I'm not bringing any baggage."

"*Je ne tiens pas à être alourdie par des bagages.*"

"*Et pas de bagages?*"

"*Par conséquent, pas de costume.*"

Luke called out; he needed toilet paper.

"Right. Maybe she'd have a piece of chiffon I could drape around myself when I get there. Just a minute." I got the paper out of the cupboard, handed it through the door and went back to the phone.

"She's got trunks all over the place with all kinds of costumes and material. Up in the *grenier*."

"What's that?"

"It's the attic. All Sean's friends sleep up there. They're kind of like the knights."

Good lord. What else hadn't she told me? A whole lot, I expected. Just a whole lot. I hung up the phone slowly. Luke finally went and got the lettuce, came in and slid the colander along the counter where I was writing the letter, and headed back to the TV. The colander hit my hand. I went and stood in his doorway again. "Some nights, you know, honey, it really helps when we make supper together. Could we just do that?" His room was a wreck, but I didn't want to bring that up now.

"I don't want salad."

"We're not having just salad. We're having rice and vegetables."

"I told you, Mom, I don't like things you have to put soya sauce on."

"Okay, we'll make hamburgers as well."

"Hamburgers again!"

"You should be so lucky. Come on."

After supper we were both in a better mood, and I suggested a game of spoon hockey on the kitchen floor. We were into the face-off for the third quarter when he said, "Why are you getting out all that stuff now?"

"Well, I was listening to this man on TV the other night and he said what you should do if you're going on a trip is pack your bag and practise being a tourist in your own town." I lined up the black checker ready for our spoons. "That way you can see if you're taking too much. Just for the heck of it, I thought I might roll up my stuff into the white bag and walk up to the avenue for a milk shake. Want to come?"

"Are you kidding? Some of my friends might see me."

"Well, ride your bike then, and I'll meet you."

"He's not going to want you to make all that much fuss, Mom. He's really not. I know all about being a son." This time when I rumpled his hair, he let me.

The next day, I drove out to my office on campus and sat at my desk, staring at the wall; I was teaching at the university on a sessional appointment, but at least I had an office. What was I doing? Was I just running around looking for support from people so I didn't have to take responsibility for a decision I knew was the wrong one? If I came down on the side of going, I would have to live with the uncertainty and take the consequences, whatever they were. At least I felt more grown-up sitting in my office.

There was a knock on the door and Terry Mahler came in. He taught in the French department and had offered to help fine-tune the letter for me.

"How does the whole thing sound in French?"

"It sounds thoughtful."

"Are you sure?" I got up and went around to look over his shoulder.

"Yeah."

"Did you find a way to say that if they don't think it's a good idea I'll understand and cancel my plans?"

"There's quite a nice way of saying that. '*Si vous trouvez que mon idée de venir n'est pas si bonne que ça, dites-le-moi; je comprendrai et j'annulerai mon vol.*' They could telephone or send a telegram. But I said if you don't hear, you'd like to come a few days ahead of time."

" '*N'est pas si bonne que ça'?* Is that something like 'if you think the idea isn't so hot'?"

"That's it."

"It doesn't sound as if they're being put in a spot?"

"No, it doesn't. Really."

I crossed over to the window and stared into the courtyard. The bottom line was that I was putting them in a spot by writing at all. How could they say no?

Terry sat down on my desk. "What's the matter? Don't you think you should?"

I shook my head. He looked at me. "Listen, this invitation is practically designed so you can make an entrance." His eyes looked a little distant under his round rimless glasses.

"Do you think so?" He was supposed to know all about the French. I turned to him, trying not to appear too eager, and allowed for the fact that he must be wanting to make it easier for me.

"And look at this." I was desperate for signs, a state that in itself is a dangerous signal. He had brought along a book about a church in Poitiers. L'église Notre-Dame.

"You should go there. The region is famous for pork. There are romanesque frescoes from the early thirteenth century in the local village. Look at them here, they're about the mystical marriage of St. Catherine, the patron saint of unmarried women. On her saint's day, her followers have to get their hair done in her honour. They get their first hairpin when they're twenty-five and a second one when they're thirty. When St. Catherine died, her body was carried by angels to the top of Mount Sinai."

"I'm a lot older than thirty."

He closed the book. "It'll be all right, Kathleen. They won't have changed, your friends."

I suddenly realized that Loesic and Jean-Paul hadn't had any guarantees when they came to London that time.

They took a risk and acted on instinct. And I did feel that I had something to offer Sean now—my house, my city, my friends. Terry's son was a student of mine—they'd be about the same age. Terry put his arm around me.

"Listen," he said. "I think you're going to have a wonderful time. I really do."

My plane left from Seattle. Gresco was astonished at the easy time we had crossing the border. Driving down, Mount Baker played its usual tricks. It was a mirage, looming up like a piece of painted scenery. The highway dashed straight past White Rock. The mountain leapt across the road only to reappear on our right.

"You two both Canadians?"

"You bet."

"Have a nice day." I accelerated and we nudged around the hill past the line of cars coming back the other way.

"That's all there is to it?"

"Pretty much."

"Do you take bookings? Do you know what it's usually like for me at these border crossings?"

"No."

"Bad. Definitely harsh."

In the motel outside Seattle, I made a supper of canned soup and a pork chop. This would be the last meal I'd have on this continent before I saw him. It would be the last time I'd wash my hair. It would be the last time I'd be on this continent without having met Sean.

TWO

3

Aboard British Midlands Air, I changed my watch to 1:00 P.M. London time. A family travelling to England for a sabbatical year in Oxford took the seats around mine with much to-do as they stored their luggage in the overhead bins. After everyone settled down and plugged in their headsets, the lights were dimmed into the half hush of a hospital. The mutter of voices was intimate and distant at the same time. I heard someone fold a newspaper, and someone else coughed. I was too anxious to concentrate on a book so I decided to reread the postcards and letters Sophie had sent me from France two years ago.

Dear Mom: Just a card from the top of the world to let you know I'm on my way. Iceland is a trip: Barbie-doll stewardesses—yellow hair, becoming blue suits. There really is a Nordic type, as distinct from a Northern type. I can see nothing but snow, sleet and U.S. air force planes from my airport vantage point. Bet you were wondering who you know in Iceland, eh? Should make it to Luxembourg by sundown, then—Paris. Love, Sophie. P.S. Had to spend a night on the floor at JFK. Jesus.

I leaned back as my neighbour's knees pushed by me. The wing flap closed. I had devoured the letters Sophie sent when she went to visit. Loesic had also sent the occasional card to say how much they were enjoying Sophie and that I should think about what special children we had.

Dear Mom: It seems like all Europe is conspiring to make my trip to the old world a nightmare. Our rickety cut-rate jet landed in Luxembourg, that enigma of a country, well after the last train had left for Paris, so I had to spend a night in Hell Hotel, an establishment manned by this sinister Wolfman Jack figure in a dusty tuxedo. The tourist brochures told me that Luxembourg was trilingual, but the Wolfman seemed to be unaware of this.

I passed the night in one of the huge ornate hotel beds tiny and petrified, trying to make long-distance phone calls, but in vain. My wake-up call came at five-thirty (jarring foreign buzz), so I got up, left the hotel forever and stumped through the dark mists to the train station. A gang of boys had arrived bright and early to harass me, dancing around trying to carry my bags. Gangs of boys are like horses and dogs, Mom, you've got to show them who's in control. Under the platform I met a goatish young pervert masturbating against the tiles. Nasty continent! I forged on. By the way, this

blue suitcase of yours keeps bursting open at all the
wrong moments . . .

When I had first read this at home, I'd huddled over
my pillow, praying she had her Mace with her. I saw her
rushing down hotel corridors, creepy men leaning against
doorjambs, and waited anxiously for the phone call to say
she had arrived safely at the Richters. When I thought
about her, I felt alternately frightened, as if she'd been
sent on a secret mission and was too young to take the
responsibility (she was), or fearful she would like it so
much she wouldn't come back, or worried her presence
would intrude on their family life and be too hard on her,
or rhapsodic at the thought that our family was on its
way to reunion at last.

Dear Mom: There we were chugging through
northern France when the dawn woke me. The
wine area was pretty, although the season was too
new for grapes. I was worn out from wrestling with
the fire and brimstone and devils in Luxembourg.
The closer I got to Paris and my brother, the more
uncomfortable I became with my appearance.
Jeans, bleached hair, everything was wrong. When
we pulled into Gare de l'Est, I wrestled my luggage
onto the platform and headed for the gate. It was a
long walk. Sean looked shockingly different from
the mental image I had of him but I recognized him
at once. A little French dandy, dressed to the nines.
Very French in demeanour but unmistakably a
Haggerty. He looks more like you than you do
yourself, but then his ears stick out like my dad's

and his mouth has that peculiar sensitive set to it. He's not tall but quite wiry. His friend was very cute. Grandpa must have looked like this at seventeen, although he wasn't a dapper Frenchman in two-tone shoes. His hair is dark and curly.

She finally sent a picture of him. He was in a Metro station, wearing his bomber jacket, leaning back slightly. It could have been my father at the same age, but with a thinner, French look. The moment I saw the picture, I knew he was part of me.

Dear Mom: This morning, Loesic and I are the only ones up though there must be some fifty-odd people asleep in the castle. We're sitting in front of the fire. She's playing solitaire; I'm writing to you. I feel like I've travelled backward and landed in the Middle Ages. Stone walls are all around. Last night I slept in a red canopied bed facing a fresco of a dragon crest. People kept on arriving, disappearing for a while and emerging in their New Year's Eve finery. There were a lot of older married women and Sean is enamoured of them, kissing their hands and whisking them around the dance floor.

After a climactic custardish cake we cleared the debris away and the teenagers began spinning disks. It hit me at once: I was to be a social cripple. I can't dance to records with a straight face, and especially not with a partner. No one could understand this except an awkward fellow wallflower named Nadine. We huddled in a corner and watched her father, a famous jazz pianist, dance with various women. "Just look at him sucking up to that woman," I understood her to say. "I hate his guts." He was a dark handsome type, very charming, always bringing us drinks and encouraging us to dance. I liked Nadine.

Loesic and Jean-Paul seem happy to have me here, feeling as they do that Sean has a certain *"besoin de ses racines."* That's me: root representative. I hope I'm adequate for the position, so important to him and everyone involved. . .

That Easter, I had sent them both presents, books. It was the first present I'd sent Sean and I fussed a long time over the paper before wrapping them both the same. For him, a book of photographs in brown sepia featuring a boy climbing the Rockies with his parents, circa 1939. *A Delicate Wilderness.* For Sophie, D. M. Fraser's *The Voice of Emma Sachs.* I rode my bike down to the post office with the presents in my knapsack, unsure about mailing them but hoping that part of him might want to hear from me. I had waited a long time for the right moment, not wanting to interfere.

When Sophie came back, she didn't want to talk much about her experience. What had happened was her secret. Occasionally she would make a comment, doling out little bits of information.

"Sean and I sit on the couch and he talks English and I talk French. We fight about it."

What couch? I wanted to say. Are there three cushions or two? What does he look like, walk like, cry like, laugh like? But I couldn't ask.

It was pretty difficult for me, Mom. When I got to Pruniers, everyone was making war whoops and calling Sean a Blackfoot. It would have made him more of an orphan, I suppose, if he'd been born out of wedlock. What have Blackfeet got to do with L.A. anyway? You said about that guy, but I was the only one who knew the truth. Sometimes I sat for hours on the bed in Sean's room looking at pictures of you and my dad. There's one photo of Sean that I line up with one of Dad; both are taken from the same angle, and Sean's and Andrew's ears stick out to the same degree. I don't know what to do. Who am I to come into this unique environment waving evidence, but if I can't, who can? Diplomacy is a lonely job, but that's who I am. Special envoy number one.

Rereading these letters on the plane, it seemed to me she was trying to keep up her spirits for my sake. It worried me, that forced bravado in her letters, suggesting she felt she had to protect me, to fix something that was not her fault. Why hadn't I seen this until now? Being at home had clearly blinded me to the obvious: I thought she'd have an exciting time, expand her horizons, but perhaps the price was too high. By making a fairy tale out of it for her, what I'd really done was mask the difficulties of the situation. Sophie could safely be sent along the path through the woods because Pruniers was at the other end, never mind that it was halfway around the world. Sophie could go over there because Loesic and I wanted the children to meet, but Sophie and Sean were both so vulnerable.

In the literature of adoption the term "role handicap" can apply to the situation of an adopted child suddenly confronted with a previously unknown aspect of his or her biological past. Sean and Sophie had not grown up as brother and sister but were being told they were. I could see the two of them standing there without a clue about how to behave. This is your brother, this is your sister. But what does this mean? both would have thought. What does that mean, my father had to be away? How can a brother or sister just appear?

Rather than putting boundaries around a manageable world for Sophie—as I imagined the Richters had done with Sean—I had tried to make her part of a story she knew nothing about. Although she was out of her depth and beyond her ability to cope, she felt it was up to her to make everything all right. I had not protected her enough, and her father had treated her casually on the rare occasions she did see him. That wise, old-young face led one of my friends to describe Sophie as a ninety-year-old midget. I remembered smiling when I heard that, thinking it was part of what made my daughter so interesting. That response was self-serving too, another construct, a safety net for me, a way of seeing her that fed my need to believe she was coping so that we all could carry on. Maybe it was lack of experience or lack of an adult partner that led me to mistake that kind of precociousness in a child for maturity.

The limbo of the middle part of the flight stretched out, the passengers flattened as if ironed. My new view of Sophie's letters undermined my confidence and made me even less sure about making this trip. The plane suddenly felt cold and I curled up by the window, pulled the inadequate blanket up to my chin and looked down at the clouds. My skin was dry. The loud whisper of the engine sounded like a fan. The person in front of me let her seat back and I propped up my bag to rest my feet, trying to trick myself into feeling comfortable enough to get back to sleep. The engine whined up a notch. A break appeared in the cloud mass. I leaned over the window trying to spot some waves, then went back to wait by the bathroom. A man across the aisle struggled awake. The bathroom door popped open and shut. Bits of music strained down the aisle. A seat belt clicked.

I returned to my seat and slept fitfully next to the balding father with his thin moustache and his daughter. I dreamt I was in a cabin up the coast with the Richters living next door. They had a small daughter; I'd given her to them as well, but I didn't know why. She kept coming over and I kept picking her up. I didn't want her to speak only French so I made a point of talking to her in English. I didn't know why I'd done this. The guilt that I'd done it again, given up another child, washed over me. Maybe it wasn't too late; I might have had to miss Sean's childhood, but maybe I didn't have to miss hers. Loesic said, "You can tell the way she's spreading her legs that she's still fitting onto your hip, not mine." I also liked a small deer that they had in their yard. "I'm sorry," Loesic told me, "but we're having it for dinner."

"How do you think we should play this one?" I asked Loesic. But my question was too subtle for her to understand and there was no one to translate. When I went back to my place, the deer was in my yard. They had lied about having it for dinner because they didn't want to give it to me.

"You want too much, Kathleen."

There were some fried potatoes on a dish. I was leaving and certainly, if I wanted, I could take the deer and the girl and the fried potatoes. But when they put it like that, of course I couldn't.

I awoke to the acrid smell of the airplane, embarrassed to be sleeping so close to people I didn't know. We straightened our clothes and grovelled for our toothbrushes in the rubble of cosmetic bags under our feet. When I got back from the bathroom, the father had put on his yellow golf sweater and was eager to make conversation over the blow-dried scrambled eggs. What he was looking forward to, he said, was riding a bicycle down the country lanes between those hedgerows.

"Great bike riding in the villages over there, all right." Oxford was home to them, he said, although they'd never go back now to stay. They'd miss the lovely wood on everyone's houses, and the mountains.

"And you, are you going to Europe on a holiday?"

"No, more like family business."

"I see."

I let my seat back, took out the invitation, turned it over to look at the drawing again. This time I saw something I hadn't noticed before. The revellers were not all in the same perspective. Two of the women were more in the foreground and both were riding unicorns. The first was older, her wide lips drawn with a couple of lines, and she had two sticks in her mouth. Recorders, I guess. The one behind was younger and was playing a violin. I wasn't sure if the second one looked like me or not, but there was no doubt the first one clearly resembled my friend, Loesic Marie Richter.

The flight attendant came down the aisle glancing from side to side checking seat belts. My eardrums hurt as we began our descent into Heathrow, for me the first time in nearly fifteen years. When we got to the gate everyone jostled in the aisle, getting down their baggage. I bent down to look through the window and check the tarmac. Cloudy and cool, it looked like. There would probably be the same dreary lines of row houses in from Heathrow to Victoria Station. Then we all began moving at once as if the door had opened into a vacuum tunnel and we were all being sucked into the airport. We struggled to get a grip on our bags and cameras and resume our roles as strangers.

I took a taxi back through Notting Hill Gate. The whole of Queensway was a Middle Eastern bazaar and the awning of the greengrocer where we used to shop resembled a tent flap with Arabic script along the sides and top. Groups of veiled women sat in the back seats of limousines. Whitely's department store, next to my old flat, was boarded up, its arched windows covered by plywood. The traffic was dense and the air thick with exhaust. In Kensington Gardens, the boy with his legs apart still stood on his blue rock. As a child I had a print of that statue in my bedroom.

At Victoria Station a sea of young people with backpacks were waiting to catch the night train. I was suddenly nervous about whether the Richters had received my letter. The phone booth had a metal hood but was right over the track, so the soundproofing made little difference. I might as well have been wearing wool gloves, the way the coins stuck. I couldn't hear the operator but I had no trouble hearing the person behind me breathing

down my neck. He had a train to catch in ten minutes and
could I hurry?

"I'm trying to place a call near Poitiers, in France."

"You don't have to shout, madam. I'll connect you to
an operator in Paris."

"Thank you." I had three quarters of an hour, but I was
afraid I wouldn't get through in time and would miss the
train. I squeezed my arm tight against my side, turned
away from the phone booth and waited. If this was a bad
time, I could stay in Europe for the three weeks and we
could meet later. I wondered what Sophie and Luke were
doing. I hoped that Luke had the prow of his sunfish
pointed into a wide clear horizon and Sophie was painting a gay kite fish and smiling her contented smile.

"*Paris. Numéro, s'il vous plaît.*"

I whipped around fast but the line went dead, wiggled
the hook up and down but no luck. My urgency to see
him now that I was on the move rushed through me like a
body of water freed from a dam. A door across the con-
course led into the connecting hotel area. If I didn't get
through that afternoon, I'd spend the night there and
keep trying until I did. The ceilings in the lobby were high
and there was an inviting telephone in a quiet alcove. The
man using it had lost all his travellers' cheques. He
wanted me to eavesdrop, I could feel it. His eyes hung
onto mine as I leaned against the counter to wait. Brush-
ing some imaginary lint off my skirt, I folded back the
address book. When the phone was free I tried again. This
time I got through.

A man answered. I had no idea who. "*Allo.*"

"*Allo, je voudrais parler à Loesic, s'il vous plaît. C'est Kath-*

leen." Whoever it was left the phone without a word. Finally he came back on.

"She can't come to the phone."

"I see."

"She says she can't speak English."

"It's okay. I'll speak in French."

"*Allo, Kathleen?*" Her voice was deep and relaxed.

"*Loesic. As-tu reçu ma lettre?*"

"*Mais oui. C'est merveilleux. Viens.*"

"*Tu es certaine?*"

"*Absolument.*"

That one word—*viens*—and the way she said it sank through what felt like layers of sand and gravel in my body and I relaxed for the first time since the whole idea was sprung on me like a gilt jack-in-the-box card that day at Sophie and Gresco's. The light in the hotel lobby seemed brighter somehow and the obliging train was leaving on schedule.

Dear Mom: It's hard to know whether you should write him or not. Between us we've skirted the whole issue of parenthood, generally referring to you as Kathleen (my mom? our mom?). At any rate, here I am, smack dab in the middle of a French family. We live in one of the best parts of Paris: Montmartre. That pinnacle of white purity, the Sacré Coeur, is flanked on three sides by the roughest pornography district around. I feel like a voyeur, skulking around in my trench coat and my baseball cap, taking pictures with my Instamatic camera. The Moulin Rouge is here, and the Folies

Bergère and a whole host of newer places called things like The Bunny Girls and Pornissimo. A little further up the hill there are lots of hookers who dress like cartoon hookers in fishnet stockings, leopard-print mini-dresses, short fur jackets and bleached bouffant wigs. I hike beyond them up to the temple from which point you can see the whole of the city stretched out below, seething and misty.

Tonight we're going somewhere known as the Catacombs. Sean's three closest buddies came over directly after supper to have the maximum group-preening time. The suspense increases as they compete for mirror space, fiddling with their shirt collars (up or down? up or down?), splashing on cologne, combing their hair this way and that. We set off for the Latin Quarter at about 10:00 P.M. More friends materialize in the Metro St.-Georges while we wait for the train. The jokes are flying thick and fast over my head. We thread our way through a thin, windy puzzle of streets. Finally we reach the manhole. The silent square is deserted except for a few lurking strangers. Sean opens the manhole cover and climbs in, beckoning me. The Catacombs lie below. Jesus! My claustrophobia comes in a sickening rush as I follow him down the ladder, driven as I am by curiosity and peer pressure. The air gets progressively stickier and closer as we climb down. After what seems about fifteen minutes we strike bottom and set off down a crumbling passageway. Sean is ahead of us, negotiating our route with some sort of torch. We're in a maze of dry sewage tunnels built, one gathers, in the

Middle Ages. They have the feel of an Egyptian tomb and are decorated with a lot of centuries-old graffiti. After some time trooping through the various narrow, low passageways, Sean leads us into a large room. The roof is supported by pillars, lit with torches and filled with young people drinking, smoking and playing tapes on ghetto blasters. One group of revellers is busy doing cave drawings at the other end of the room. It seems I've come upon the most exclusive nightclub in Paris.

Once I wrote and asked Sophie how a mediaeval woman would look lying in bas-relief on her tomb. She wrote back that she would have her hands folded on her chest and no pupils in her eyes. On a beach near White Rock where we'd gone on a picnic, Gresco had pointed out what looked like a flotilla of feathers on the water. Sophie still—but as a joke now—looked for things that fit into our imaginary nation of miniature people with pointed shoes and bluebell hats. The wind opened little doors in the parchment bark of the arbutus trees. The flotilla of curved feathers floated on their tips like sailboats and the passengers dined on pancakes of sea foam. Our ritual game reminded me of one we played in high school. First you had to count red convertibles. Once you reached a hundred, you started on the yellows. Then the whites. The first boy you saw after you had counted fifty whites was the one you were going to marry. Where are you on your convertibles? we would say.

On the night boat, a little blond boy kept shouting and running about. His parents didn't seem to care and acted as if he were the only kid aboard and it didn't matter if anyone else wanted to sleep. I knew the Richters wouldn't have brought Sean up like that. A handsome bony woman with thin hair collapsed on the bench next to me, kicked off her shoes and curled up using her purse as a pillow. We slept for a little while with our hair touching. Suddenly she sat bolt upright. "Will you please silence that child?" His parents looked right through her.

"These idiotic people think they're some kind of nobility," she muttered. Her voice startled the boy, who would have sat down and shut up if his parents hadn't condoned his behaviour by ignoring her.

"Damn Scandinavians. It's so typical. They'll never stop colonizing. Iceland, now here. I never get any rest." She lay down as suddenly as she had sat up and went back to sleep.

I went to the cafeteria and bought three green plums and saved one to offer her when she woke up. The young people I had seen back at the station were camped in the ship's discothèque, backpacks and bodies slumped against the wall. At Dunkirk, in the small of the night, waiting for the train to leave, the bony woman and I took seats opposite each other and shared a sandwich. She was an archaeologist going to the south of France on a dig. What looked to me like steam from the train's engine turned out to be fog. "If it hadn't been for the fog," the archaeologist said, "the Germans would have seen there were no soldiers on the beaches. The fog was like a gift from God, so the Luftwaffe had to bomb at random." She looked out the window sadly. The early dawn cast a green tinge, a metallic mud tone on a second train waiting on the track beside ours.

Finally Paris. I was half asleep as I made my way down

the platform in the muggy air. Not expecting Sean at the gate, I thought I saw him anyway among the crowds of young people rushing about the station. I'd forgotten how huge the Gare d'Austerlitz was. Someone beside me was wearing that eau de cologne from the lemon bottle with the turquoise label and I knew I was back in Europe. Outside the station the streets were being washed. A pneumatic drill started up and fresh baking smells drifted in from the back of the shops. I wandered over to the botanical garden next to the station and found a bench. It was the first time I'd been able to stretch out in two days. I lay on my side with my head on my pack and couldn't keep my eyes off the children playing in the park. Had he worn that kind of smock? Had he played here? I rolled onto my back and pulled my newspaper over my face. I couldn't keep up with the conversations I heard and it seemed to me suddenly that Paris was an old beauty who had nothing to do with me.

"*Un billet pour Poitiers, s'il vous plaît.*"
"*Comment?*"
I was trying to talk to the ticket agent and felt he understood me but was pretending not to. At the information booth the person spoke more slowly and said, yes, they did have a system. Ten minutes before the train leaves, they post the track.

What you have to do, Mom, is step way back so you can see the board above the train track. You'll be sure they're never going to post the Poitiers train, but then they will and you'll have to rush for it.

I worried about the connecting train at Poitiers and even thought perhaps it wouldn't be too far to take a taxi if I had to. *Combien pour aller jusqu'au village?* At Tours, in the train's washroom, I put some face powder on the bags under my eyes. Back at my seat, my luggage appeared to have been moved to the seat across from me. How did that happen? Did the train get turned around? I never rode backwards. As the train pulled out it was headed, by my reckoning, back to Paris. I saw the conductor and asked, *"Le prochain arrêt?"*

"Poitiers."

When I arrived in Poitiers, I called Loesic, who didn't sound at all surprised I had made it this far. Could someone meet me? Someone, apparently, could. If I hadn't been so tired and anxious I would have been charmed by the trip. The train wandered through the vegetable gardens of the local villages; people had their tomatoes trained around stakes and almost all the leaves pulled off, which surprised me. I always left the leaves on to keep the fruit from scorching. There were tubs of red geraniums beside the blue doors of each whitewashed station. After a dozen local stops, the third train I'd taken in two days stopped at the Richters' village and I waited for the door to open. Please God, I prayed, don't let me overplay this.

4

I spotted Loesic leaning against the station doorway. She had gained a little weight but otherwise looked so much the same that I bolted straight off the train into her arms. She bundled me into the car quickly as if my reappearance were a sleight of hand trick and no one at the station was meant to see me, turned the wheel sharply and skidded out of the yard. "*Ça va, Kathleen?*"

"*Très bien, et toi?*"

"*Très bien, très occupée, mais très bien.*"

"*Et Sean?*"

"*Très bien.*"

She swerved out the gate and drove rapidly through the countryside, still with those powerful shoulders and the cigarette in the corner of her mouth. The smoke made the corners of her eyes crinkle. She looked older, not that much older but older, with lines around her eyes that she hadn't had before, and her hair was greyer. She drove so quickly that I had to keep looking back over my shoulder out of nervousness. If this was difficult for her, she didn't show it. But it must be. It must be.

There was something bothering her about our son—she said *notre fils*. It was almost as if we had just discussed him yesterday and were now continuing the conversation, the way she said it, trying to normalize things, which made me love her. What was bothering her most about our son was that he had military service coming up and he was not at all the type for military service. I'd forgotten they had conscription in France. But we shouldn't worry, she said.

Shouldn't we?

No, because he wants to be a *cinéaste*.

A what? It was already going way too fast. All I could think about now was seeing him. When? How many more minutes? What's he thinking? Is he as scared as I am? *"Un homme qui fait des films?"*

"Oui."

"A producer or director?"

"Director."

We came to a stop sign, but she didn't really stop, just geared down, looked both ways and then bolted off again. I was clutching the seat, panicked. Narrow roads, hedges, gentle hills. Grapevines, old wooden doorways outlined by stones, houses tucked into the sides of hills. She took her cigarette out of her mouth and changed gears, put it back in the other side of her mouth.

"Sometimes they don't make them learn combat. They give them other things to do. Maybe they'll let him make propaganda films." She laughed at this, as if it were both preposterous and hilarious that he could do such a thing. Why was her French so easy to understand and everyone else's so difficult? I looked over at her without seeing her.

"He might not even have to learn to use a gun. Unless he wants to."

"I see."

"And I don't think he does. You'll see. He's not the type." I remembered she had said, even before she left London, that she would tell Sean that what we were doing was normal, that in some other cultures such arrangements were taken as a matter of course. Because of our own laws and customs, there were no rules or guidelines for people in our situation, and so we had to invent them. Would he have believed that? Would it have meant anything to him? Would she actually have *said* any of that to him? I wanted to ask her if there was anything special I should say or not say, but the question was too difficult for my limited French. Look at yourself as you would at another person, and then tell that person what to do, I said to myself. Aunt, try aunt.

The closer we got, the more nervous I felt. I was almost there but he was as far away as he'd always been, because I hadn't met him yet.

"*Ça va Sophie?*"

"*Très bien.*"

"*Et Lucas?*"

"*Très bien aussi.*"

"*Et ta mère?*"

"*Elle est bien. C'est tout que je peux dire. Très bien.*"

She smiled, she remembered.

Then all at once we turned into a wide driveway, drove past some stone outbuildings and pulled smack up against the front of their place. It felt as though we had parked too close to the castle, and I peered up at it from under the windshield. It was built on the side of a hill with a deep gulley and field below. The heavy double door was sunk into a recess with a knoll in front. Nobody could be in there, it was too old and far away. In mediaeval times, the castle was the whole world—home, church, prison, blacksmith shop, dungeon.

"*C'est ça? Chez toi, eh?*"

She nodded. I looked at her and suddenly remembered her telling me in London that not having a child had been like a death sentence to her. Their leaving in the taxi from Bennington Gardens and my arrival at Pruniers spliced for me at this second and there was no space in between. I sat there frozen as if I had turned into the kind of statue you'd expect to find in a place like this, unable to imagine actually going inside.

Crenellated, that's what it's called, where the top of the wall juts up and down like jack-o'-lantern teeth. It was dusk and the moon had risen over one of the towers in a sky that hadn't quite paled; it was the colour of skin grown over a blood blister. Loesic jumped out and opened the trunk as I slowly got out of the car, still looking up at the chateau. I reached in for my bag and Loesic took my hand from where it visored my eyes, tucked it under her arm and pulled me with her through the front door, along a stone corridor down a wide dark hall where the stones in the cobbled floor came right up to meet my feet; we tromped past a heavy oak table and into a large kitchen with a tile floor. The light was gutted low and I could see people sitting around the sides of the room, some at a long table, some standing along the walls and others over by the fireplace. She steered me towards a group of boys, young men really, some on a grouping of sofas, some standing by a casement window. How was I going to know which one was him? But there he was coming up out of the group, slim, head to one side, arms turned slightly outwards in their sockets, one shoulder dropped and back. He stood right in front of me, my younger self as a boy staring up at me. No, someone else altogether staring at me. His older self as a woman must be staring back at him. Sophie had said we looked alike but I didn't expect this much. He walked straight into my arms, smiling. I knew those teeth, that nose, that hair, and there he was.

There he was.

"Sean, Kathleen. Kathleen, Sean."

His cheek against mine, arm's length. Looking from this angle and that, arm's length again. I couldn't take it all in, dark frames then strobe lights, speeded up now. My senses got mixed up, my breath in my eyes. Holding shoulders, looking from this angle, that. Nothing else existed, just him, me, my flesh catching with his again; nothing was there, no one was there except him. The lights came on. We were laughing and crying at the same time. I wanted to touch his temples, smooth back the brown curly hair plastered down at the sides. A little more distant, his eyes the same pale brown as Sophie's. Widely set like hers. Loesic started to laugh as Jean-Paul burst in, chest bulging out of his overalls, pleasure bursting out of his face. "Kathleen!"

His arms thrashed past mine. Then we were all laughing and crying at the same time and I couldn't take my head off Loesic's shoulder. I said it had been a long, long way, I was so tired, that's why I was crying. Sure, she said. Sure.

He had to introduce me to his friends: I met and shook

hands with everybody—Claude, Poupon, Eric. He picked
up my bag and backed out into the corridor, pushing his
shoulder against the door. A mounted deer head leaned
against the wall where we had come in. We climbed up a
wide stone staircase, grabbing quick looks at each other,
laughing when we realized we were both doing the same
thing. I glanced back inside the room at Loesic and Jean-
Paul but they just waved us on. When we got to the top of
the stairs, he took my chin in his hand, turned my head to
one side, leaned his head back and peered at my nose. I
tightened my eyelids against the numbing at the bridge of
my nose that meant more tears, held my breath in
snatches. More nervous laughter as we turned into a vast
banquet room with a tall wardrobe at one end. An enor-
mous painting done like a tapestry covered the wall. We
crossed a stone threshold into a bedroom with a carved
chest up against a long expanse of white wall and a trestle
table with a giant half-completed jigsaw puzzle, through
to another bedroom and up a staircase to another floor.
All the furniture was old and carved—long tables with
candelabras, more chests, period and modern tapestries.
He lit the candles in brackets up and down the hall and I
followed him around corners, past recessed nooks. In the
top-floor bedroom stood a headless dress dummy wearing a half-finished net dress decked with silver paper
fans. He closed the door gently and put a finger to his
lips.

"Do you come here often?" I whispered.

"*Oui. Pâques, Nöel, tout l'été.*"

"All summer? Every year?"

"*Oui.*"

"You're lucky."

He opened the door on the last flight of stairs to the grenier to show me the towers from the inside as we kept looking at each other and talking and walking through a room almost half the size of a soccer field. Around the back of the stairs, a raised platform was blocked off with white muslin curtains. Rows of single mattresses lay side by side; more net partitions draped the sleeping areas. A turret faced in each direction—north, south, east and west. Back downstairs we came into the oldest part, a single turret like a castle in a chess set. There was an old carved wooden fireplace on one wall; on the opposite wall, facing the bed, the fresco with lions and fleur-de-lys, the stones gutted and damp, the walls so thick that an insert of broad tiles under the window formed a deep window seat. He wasn't as tall as I thought he'd be. I'm so used to the smells and textures of Luke's and Sophie's bodies because I've touched them so many times; I should know all those details about Sean, but he felt slightly out of reach, as if I were a child who'd never been allowed to touch or explore her environment and had grown up not knowing the feel of the most familiar things. He didn't look scared at all, happy and assured really. Just wanting me to see everything so badly. A layer of my skin began warming into an existence I hadn't known was there.

At last we came to his room and he put my bag down on the same canopied bed I had slept in at Bouchauds in 1966. He sat down on the bed and zipped open my bag. What was he looking for, a present? I'd brought one—a green satin robe and a portfolio of family pictures—but he found what he wanted, the mirror from my cosmetic bag. He took out a mascara tube, pulled the stopper, examined it and put it back. Took out a lipstick, opened the tube, closed it and put it back. Then he examined himself in the compact mirror, closed it, put it back. Finally, he zipped up the cosmetic bag, then the bigger bag, and threw his hand up at the room.

"*C'est ma chambre. C'est ta chambre.*"

"Are you sure? Where are you going to sleep?"

"*Dans le grenier. Avec mes amis.*"

"Is that okay?"

"No, it's good."

He walked over to the window, set into a bay by the thickness of the walls, and stared down at a field between the castle and the outbuildings. The end of his nose and bow of his mouth pulled forward a little when he was concentrating and, in profile, a lot of the whites of his eyes showed. He stared straight ahead to the door on the chapel where Sophie said they kept the rakes and the lawn mower.

Smoke from the fireplace filled the room, making my eyes water. He turned and looked straight at me. "Why didn't you come before, Kathleen?"

"I wanted to, Sean. I wanted to many times but I stopped myself because I thought it would be too confusing for you when you were little to have two mothers." I don't know where my French came from but it was there. It had to be there. "I've been waiting for this day for eighteen years."

He looked pleased and uncertain at the same time, and I just tried to stay quiet and matter-of-fact and there. I kept wanting to reassure him but I couldn't think how. He had no reason to trust me. All I could do was sit there worrying that Jean-Paul and Loesic would think we'd been gone too long.

"Je descends, Kathleen. I'm going down now."
"Oui."

The rush of joy left with him. Suddenly I didn't know what to do, like in my dream where the children had no arms or legs and I was back, empty, in the recovery room, the whole tenuous beginning sucked out from under me.

Might as well unpack. Where had he gone? What was he doing? I knew I was going to want to keep running after him—not let him out of my sight—but I shouldn't act on that, like they said when I was having him, don't push now, not yet. Kind of a cloistered place, this room. I laid my things out on the bed. Skirt, T-shirt, cardigan, a pair of pants, that was it. I should have brought more clothes. I folded my T-shirt over and over. Even a piece of paper only folds eight times. Started out the door. Stopped myself. He was gentle, nice. I liked him. Opened the door of the wardrobe. A man's pink cotton shirt. Must be his. Nice shirt. Held it up to my chest, then to my cheek, put it back and went right up close to the fresco to see what kind of fixative they'd used. Layers of shellac, it looked like. Imagine sleeping in a room with a fresco painted before Shakespeare was born. Holy smokes. *Nom d'une pipe.* I ran my hand along the window seat. Needed a couple of cushions. What was he doing back downstairs? Had his friends cordoned him off back in the corner against the ropes and put a towel around his shoulders? Was this long enough? Time enough for them to regroup? An easel holding a portfolio of prints stood beside the window. I leafed through them, leaning my head to one side to look at an etching. The cherry tree branches at

Bouchauds? Perhaps. It had taken so much to get there and now I had to wait again, trailing my fingers along the high-backed wooden chair, drumming on the armrest. What did you do with Kathleen, Sean? *Elle est fatiguée. Elle est très fatiguée.* She's gone to bed. *Vraiment? Oui.* A tactful interlude. *Je descends aussi.* You're coming down too? In a minute, yes.

When I came into the kitchen, everyone fell silent. I looked around for him. He wasn't there and I panicked again, thinking I'd made a terrible mistake. I was too tired to speak English, let alone French, but I kept trying until Loesic suggested kindly maybe I really should go to bed. A lot of people were hanging around the foyer. Where was Sean? Out in the theatre with the mummers. The mummers? I looked for him in the crowd, around corners, but I couldn't find him. In the salon, a woman sang one line of a song over and over. *The boat is in the harbour. I can't pay the rent.* Practising for the fête? I wondered whatever happened to Niki. Ridiculous cosmic sixties. *It's all meant to be, Kathleen.* Sure.

I found him finally in the theatre. He and Jean-Paul were climbing up and down ladders hanging stacks of identically painted sleeves cut from styrofoam, and each cut-out gloved hand held a stick with a face like a sun, the faces surrounded with points. I didn't call up to him or anything, just turned away, knowing that the right thing to do was just go to bed. But in bed I was too tired to sleep: I lay awake staring at the gold-threaded pattern on the canopy. He must have looked at this ceiling day and night since he was a little boy. Go to sleep, I told myself, just go to sleep. He'll be there in the morning.

Morning, and the women of Pruniers whispered in the next room. Gold-dipped roses in a vase, gold threads in the pillow. Smell of toast. Sunlight poured through the narrow slits in the wall. I thought they must be for ventilation but Sophie told me later they were for shooting arrows through. (Lucky they're too small to admit outside arrows, she said.)

"There's the Turkish vest with gold trim. She could sew elastic around the ankles."

"Does she sew?"

"Oh, she sews."

I drifted back to sleep and woke to the smell of fresh tomatoes and basil. Men's voices shouted from the soccer field below. A Nile-green chiffon tunic dress with wide legs and an embroidered Turkish vest hung from the doorknob of the wardrobe, elastic for the pants looped around the neck. I wanted to get up. I wanted to see him as soon as I could.

Theatrical light bulbs bordered the mirror in the bathroom. An ironing board was balanced on the edge of the tub on one end and the sink on the other. A short woman with a double chin, rosebud mouth and blonde-white hair softer and younger than her skin was sewing fabric flowers around the wire support of a butterfly headdress, one of those mediaeval affairs that arch above the ears so your rolled-under hair is caught in a loosely woven net. There was someone in a novel who got headaches from a headdress like that. I remember she was advised to get rid of the scaffolding and, once she did, her headaches disappeared, her smile was young again, her eyes clear blue. The woman sewing the flowers introduced herself as

Marie-Claire, Loesic's best friend. Last night when I was meeting everyone, Loesic had had her arm around Marie-Claire and called her her sister. Sophie, in one of her letters: "At the New Year's party, Loesic introduced me as her daughter. The guest looked at us and nodded. Ah, yes, they saw the family resemblance." I smiled hesitantly and she smiled back but didn't move the ironing board so I left to find another bathroom.

There were stashes of glitter and pots of make-up along the window sills and on top of bureaus. Baskets of fabric flowers and bolts of chiffon lay on the dresser. *Y aurait-il peut-être un morceau de tissu que je pourrai draper autour de ma personne?* I padded along in my bare feet with my cosmetic bag. Trunks and wardrobes spilled over with more costumes. Satin pyjamas, kimonos, checked harlequin tights. More *morceaux de tissu.* In another dressing room down yet another corridor, I came across Loesic setting out piles of rosettes and coils of gold string.

"Merci pour le costume, Loesic. C'est très beau." I looked at her hesitantly.

"De rien, chérie."

She hugged me—kissed me on both cheeks—it was weird hugging and kissing in the morning with a full bladder and your teeth unbrushed. I asked about another bathroom and she pointed me upstairs. Someone was in the shower so I settled to wait beside another old trunk filled with blue taffeta open at the casement window. The window looked down into the courtyard, and suddenly Sean came whistling down the path pushing a wheelbarrow full of glass jars. One shoulder was bent back, the other leading. He looked even slimmer-hipped than he had last night; I could watch him without him knowing and tried to remember which of his shoulders came out of me first. Watching him lean down, I moved my own shoulders back and forth.

He stopped at a pile of sand beside the chapel door, picked up a small shovel and began spading the sand into the jars, digging the sand in an odd, inefficient way with his wrist loose, levering the shovel from the elbow instead of using his whole arm. When he was distracted, the end of his nose and the point of his mouth retracted. Did mine do that? I leaned over, my arms spread along the sill of rough tiles, and peered down, reaching back for a chair. Odd, it wasn't a chair but an antique double-seated wheelbarrow. Either it was made for children or people were a lot smaller in those days. Ladies with alabaster skin and thin eyebrows. You didn't get to have eyelashes either, only deep lids and a high forehead, but you had high coiled wings of hair and veils that fell from the tips of cone hats and those flat bodices that dropped in a boned V between your legs. A figure spinning on a distaff drifted down the hall, glancing over her shoulder, her cupped hat held in place by a white scarf with the ends floating behind her. She held her distaff under one arm like a broom, and a thread, held gingerly between her little finger and her thumb, stretched like a spider filament across her black apron.

Dear Mom: Today I sat in each of the towers one at a time with my arms around my knees. The roofs sat on my head like caps. From where I could see in each direction, there was nothing to make me think I wasn't in the Middle Ages. . .

Small shovel or not, inefficient or not, he managed a large heap of sand in a pretty short time. He put down the spade, covered his face with his hands, leaned over and retched. Good lord, what's wrong with him? I stood up. He tried again, but nothing came out. Just then the bathroom door swung open and Jean-Paul emerged whistling, glowing from the steam, a towel wrapped around his hips.

"Jean-Paul, what's wrong with him?" I pulled him to the window.

"Nothing's wrong with him." He looked at me wondering what I was talking about. When I looked back down, Sean had gone back to his digging as if nothing had happened.

Jean-Paul curled the wire hooks of his glasses over one ear, then the other. He had more lines in his face too, and that ruddiness could mean high blood pressure. He stood there with his towel wrapped around his hips watching his son.

"*Il est très beau, hein?*"

"He sure is."

"Now that you see him, Kathleen, who would you say is the father?"

"How do you mean?"

He didn't seem bothered by the question, just matter-of-factly wanted to know.

"Are you sure he's all right?"

"Of course he's all right."

"*Andrew, bien sûr.*"

"You're that sure?"

"I'm one hundred per cent sure."

"We thought it was the Blackfoot." He looked disappointed.

"No."

Didn't he remember that time on the river at Bouchauds? Perhaps those memories didn't have as much impact for them. Maybe they hadn't understood me. I had tried to tell them. Or maybe they didn't want to hear me. Sean picked up the empty wheelbarrow and wheeled it off.

"I told you when he was a few months old and I came to Bouchauds that time. When we did the papers. We were on the river."

"We always thought it was that Indian guy."

"No."

White porcelain busts of a variety of strange people stared out from the bathroom wall, accusing me. Boxes of pink tissue sat on the toilet lid. There was no water for the shower so I made do with a tepid sponge bath, then did my best with my appearance. Running my hands over my hips to straighten my skirt, I headed down to the kitchen where a group of people were making lunch. I didn't see Sean. A bowl of coffee and a piece of toast were set out for me by the fireplace. I sat quietly on the hearth seat, aware that I was the stranger and had to get the lay of the land and let people get used to me.

Lunch at the long table was going to be for at least thirty. Crates of celery, tomatoes, zucchini and pears were stacked on the counter. A mountain of potato salad in an outsize bowl weighed down the sideboard. Cakes and pies were piled up in the bedroom behind the kitchen. A thin man with a pale face tied a white apron over his jeans, separated half a dozen eggs and began to whisk the whites. Loesic put her hand on his arm and leaned over, smiling, to see what he was doing.

"Not so rich as the other night, Gilbert, okay?"

The people who were invited to the fête appeared to be creating it.

The raised hearth was close to the floor. It was cold, and I was about to get up and find a pillow when I felt a solid warmth beside me shoving me over, a wide black velour hip and Loesic slid alongside me, pressing her back up against the stones. She tucked my hair behind my ears and I returned her gaze over the rim of my bowl.

"*Je suis très contente que tu sois ici, Kathleen.*" She looked me straight in the eye; I knew she wasn't saying this because it was what I wanted to hear, not altogether.

I had thought that Sean's living in France, so far away and with a different language and customs, would make a difference, would make it easier, but it never had; I don't think one day passed that I didn't think of him, feel a cold wind through my body. I realized Loesic must have known eighteen years before that maybe I was not in any condition to make the decision I did. But it had been the right decision. That seemed clear. I didn't know how to begin to thank them for what they had done. Her face settled into the quiet repose of someone who knew how to make contact where it counted.

"*Sean, est-il malade ce matin?*"

"*Mais non.*"

"*Oui, je pense . . .*"

She shrugged. She wasn't worried. If he were really sick, her look seemed to say, she'd know about it.

She went over to the table, picked up a peach from the bowl and came back with it in the palm of her hand.

"*Cette pêche, elle doit mûrir.*" It had to ripen. "*Je ne suis pas possessive avec Sean.* He is his own person; it's time for him to start reaching out on his own. You've come at exactly the right time."

While she was saying this she saw something going on in the cooking that bothered her. She went over to put her finger in a bowl of batter a young woman in a purple Mickey Mouse T-shirt was stirring. She tasted it and said, "*Un peu de sucre.*"

At the time of the adoption my impression of Loesic was a projection of my own wishful thinking, a case of finding virtue in necessity. I knew that. I knew it was sheer luck that she had turned out to be the person I imagined her to be, and I was wishful thinking again now. No matter what others might say, I couldn't rationalize away the fact that on one level I was imposing. But here I was.

She came back and reached down her hands. "More than that, I've never forgotten you." So. I was not to sit over here by myself. She wanted to introduce me to everyone. People were taking their seats at the long table, laughing and throwing bread at each other, leaping up to swat flies.

"*C'est Kathleen,*" she announced to everyone. "*La mère de mon fils.*" She laughed. They all laughed. She was at ease, which put her friends at ease. I didn't know what to say. Loesic didn't have a bourgeois bone in her body. Neither of them did. I did, though. I no longer took pleasure from the outlandish or the bizarre. It made me feel as if I were compensating for something. Clearly what she was saying was that she trusted me to make the right moves with him and behave in a way that would fit in.

How Jean-Paul might have felt was a little harder to figure out.

The two of them sat side by side at the head of the table, but Sean was not beside them. I kept looking for him. The ceiling was beamed and low and dark except for the rectangles of the windows casting light on the broad planked table. Loesic stood up and rapped a glass with a spoon. Would everyone remember to soap themselves before they got in the shower and please would they use only a little water? Glitter, make-up and headdresses were available in the third- and fourth-floor bathrooms. Guests might be asked to leave their rooms between two and three for a guided tour of men from the local rest home. That's how Loesic and Jean-Paul paid for the upkeep of the place, explained my neighbour, the pale man called Gilbert, who translated all this for me—they got a tax deduction in exchange for providing tours.

Would Sean be coming to lunch? She didn't know. And now would someone please pass her the cauliflower in cream and onion sauce? Would they hand over the hot pork roast, the sweet green grapes and the excellent peaches?

After lunch, I started to clear the table and do the dishes but someone took the dish rag out of my hands. Someone would come to do them later. All right then, what about the flowers? A bouquet on the pedestal in front of the main staircase where I first came in? In an urn? Why not? There was a bouquet already in the spot I had in mind, but it had wilted.

Loesic lifted the flowers from the vase and spread them on some newspapers. I began to wrap them up to throw out, but she stopped me and sorted out the ones that were still usable. She smiled, looked around for the next job, then started back into the kitchen for something, couldn't remember what. She pushed her elbows back, put her head to one side, pursed her mouth for a second try and charged in again, stopping to have a polka up and down the kitchen with a little girl wearing a net petticoat and a tinfoil crown. Back in the hall, armed with clippers, she led me out the door and there was Sean, coming across the field between the theatre and the castle. Loesic raised a hand in greeting, not stopping to speak although Sean turned towards her. I wished she would. I didn't want him to think she was withdrawing from him because I was there. But perhaps I was being overly sensitive and she was just preoccupied. Sean recovered almost instantly. How had my night been?

My night was fine. How was his? Really fine. How was he today? In fact, he was quite well, but not really well. He had *mal à la gorge*—he touched his throat—and had been busy all morning in the theatre with the strobe lights. Lunch was a ham sandwich on the run. He cocked his head. Come and see the lights. I nodded in the direction of the hollyhocks where Loesic was waiting for me. Ah, *plus tard* then. He walked along with me instead. Did I know that they were expecting dozens of people for the fête and they would all be sleeping overnight, wasn't it exciting? One family planned to arrive in a wooden horse. Really? So it was not the best time in the world to have a sore throat. No. I had some throat lozenges in my purse, an embroidered shoulder bag that Loesic sent Sophie years ago. Would he like one? He would. "Maybe you should have a nap, *un petit dodo*?" He took a lozenge from the top of the package and walked off to the house. Oh, no, I bet that's baby talk, *un petit dodo*. Too late now. Loesic waited patiently by the hollyhocks.

"He has a sore throat. I gave him some lozenges."

"*Oui.*"

In the entranceway, the little girl, Simone, was sucking and nibbling the stem of one of the flowers on the newspaper and singing a song about *la gladiola*. Loesic and I chose this colour and that from the flowers we had cut, standing back to decide where they should go. Holding a thick stem like a dart, I aimed it at the vase. Strange ancient iron devices were arrayed on a table by the door.

"What are these for, Simone?"

She took a blossom from a stem and stuck it down the front of her dress.

"*La torture.*"

"*Pardon?*"

"*La torture.*"

"*Ah.*"

Jean-Paul, his naked chest hairy under his overall bib, pushed a wheelbarrow filled with jars of sand past the open front door. The entrance hall of the castle where Simone and I were misting the flower arrangement was dark and cool. He passed by in glaring sunlight. He let go the handles of the wheelbarrow, took a handkerchief from his pocket and wiped his face.

"Fifteen years on this fucking castle," he said in his careful English. "And fifteen more to go."

He picked up the handles and pressed on.

Later that afternoon, when I was in my room putting in my contact lenses, Sean rapped at the door, then rushed to the next room like a town crier. We were all to leave our rooms while the tour came through. I crouched at the top of the main staircase and peered down at the backs of the men from the local rest home, all dressed in the same soft blue shirts and shapeless trousers. Loesic carefully explained the torture instruments on the table in the entranceway and, that time, I couldn't understand one word of her French. One by one the men turned their heads slowly and opened their mouths, looking up the staircase to stare at me where I waited at the top of the stairs, listening to her.

5

The next day at lunch a dish of casaba melon was passed around.

"If this place gets too expensive," Jean-Paul announced, "we'll go to Canada to visit Kathleen. Ha ha."

People passed the dish along without really looking at it. It was part of the first course, to go with the ham. I took two slices and handed the platter to the next person. Loesic reached over and took one slice off my plate. "Everyone gets one," she said.

When she said that, the bottom fell out. All the stress and tension of the situation suddenly overwhelmed me and I excused myself quietly and went upstairs to my room. The children here came up so close when they talked to you. How did they feel when they'd never seen you before and they had to kiss you in the mornings? Sean had Andrew's face and Sean had Dad's face and my dad hadn't trusted Andrew.

I sat on the edge of the bed, shaking. There was a knock on the door and Gilbert, the man with the pale face, came in. At lunch he'd translated for me, passing me sentences along with the dishes without anyone seeming to notice what he was doing. He must have been the one who answered the phone when I called from London.

"I'm sorry," I said to Gilbert.

"It's all right. Everyone understands."

"Will there be speeches at dinner? Should I say something?"

Another knock. This time it was Sean. Gilbert hesitated, unsure whether to stay and translate or leave. He left and I sat up and reached for the shirt in the cupboard.

"Is it okay if I put on this shirt?"

"Of course."

"I didn't mean to . . ."

"It's okay."

"I don't want you to think . . ."

"I know, I don't think."

"You're so much a part of this place and I think . . ."

"Well, don't. Don't think anything." This time when he reached over, his mouth followed onto my cheek and then his body was in my arms and it was all I could do to look up at the ceiling and go on holding him at the same time.

"I know all about what happened. You don't have to explain." He was managing much better tonight in English than I had last night in French.

"Do you?"

"Yes. You were all alone. Your husband had left, yes? Sophie's father?"

"Andrew. He thought there was a possibility you were not his."

"So he wanted me to be his?"

"I expect he did, yes."

"It's funny. Sophie told me he was an actor and I

always wanted to be an actor, but I couldn't bring myself to put my face in front of people."

"Sophie told you?"

"I just didn't know where it came from, the acting. It wasn't anything like my parents. I guess you thought if you gave me to my parents, he might come back?"

"I'm afraid that was part of it. We could have gone back to Spain, you and me and Sophie, but I don't know how well we would have managed without Jean-Paul and Loesic. I still don't know. I'll always wonder."

"That's true." He settled back against the pillow.

"Have you known about me for a long time?"

"I have, you know, Kathleen. Maman began to tell me about my . . . double life before I think I could even understand her words. She told me, how do you say *graduellement*?"

"Gradually."

"Yes, she told me gradually. She told me that before she had the pleasure of meeting you, she almost had the pleasure of meeting Mr. or Mrs. Death, I don't know which one. Jean-Paul had to drive her around Paris in a taxi looking for a hospital with a bed and she nearly bled to death. And then she had a—what do you call it—a hysterectomy? She said that she had to have the place where I would have lived taken out of her body, so it was lucky that you had room for me in your body until she could come to get me in London." He looked at me and then looked away.

"That was a good way to put it."

"But I'm not a child now."

"No."

He turned on his side, cheek on the pillow. "So, when

you think about it, in a way it was because of Niki coming there?"

"In a way, yes."

"But if she hadn't come to Bouchauds?"

"If, a lot of things. If I'd stayed in Spain . . ."

"But, Kathleen, it's not a useful word, if. We shouldn't say it."

I sighed. "No, but we do."

Another knock at the door. It was Marie-Claire with a heavy petal headdress I was supposed to pin to the back of my head. I didn't want him to go but he left to get ready and I began to assemble my costume. I put on my cardigan against the chill and made my way downstairs and across the field. A group of people I hadn't seen before were sitting in rows in the old dovecote, whose front had crumbled away. Candles sunk in glass jars full of sand were scattered all over the yard. A dog barked. In the centre of the field where I had given Sean the lozenge, Gilbert bent down to light the first of the fireworks. He was dressed in a black bodysuit. The front view of his skeleton was painted on his back so that when he bent over he seemed to be doing a back bend. His friend Fred wore a harlequin costume, his face painted white, even his lips; he stood quietly over the skull gaping up at him, silently handing Gilbert lit matches.

A line of mummers shuffled in across the hay-strewn yard under the overhanging eaves of the theatre where the tables were set for dinner. First, a figure in baggy pants with bells at his waist, then a monkey playing a drum, then an ogre with fangs. A man with a cowl walked up with a tray, offering drinks, then a parade of ladies with large white handkerchiefs folded over the scaffolded frames of their headdresses arrived and parked their cars at the gates. Although some figures were in smaller proportion than others, it was a tapestry come to life, the figures all painted on the same plane. A robed man with a bunched-up hat pushed forward on his brow leaned over to talk to an abbot the size of a child. A rabbit with cocked ears sat in the sky where the moon should be. Hundreds of carefully woven lilies of the valley, bluebells and columbine rained down from the sky. Across the way, beside the door to the dining hall, Sean, in a folded tunic and pants cut from a kind of flimsy gold paper fabric, a wide cummerbund and shoes turned up at the toes, greeted his guests.

A row of Chinese lanterns hung from the eaves of the roof where Loesic stood decked out in a dress of the same material as Sean's tunic. The material looked so flimsy and temporary that I suddenly realized the whole event was a send-up. Loesic had kept her glasses on and was still in her work boots. Jean-Paul's tunic was cut from the same fabric but he wore his regular trousers, which only reached the top of his socks above his oxford shoes. The scene was at once both more artificial and more casual than I had expected, more a suggestion than an enactment. There was a tired-looking horse with green eyes. A fool shook his bells in my ear. One Esmeralda carried a goat in her arms, the other didn't. Loesic had mounted the oddest contraption on top of her head, a globe of wires forming a small cage with a gilt rose placed inside. She put her hand on top of the headdress and told me that the rose had been a shrivelled bud until one day a prince came along and unfastened the latch on the door, and suddenly it burst into full bloom.

Several ladies carrying distaffs like batons under their arms came by with their hands over their mouths to hide their laughter. They twirled their threads while talking to a blacksmith bent over his anvil and a carpenter leaning on his adze. People were working and talking, eating and talking, playing music and talking. The frog lady who wanted to be as big as a cow—she had black lips and a wide tadpole over her crotch—shrank into a miniature only to reappear under the hem of a demoiselle whose goat's front legs twined around the pole of her tent. A lion spouted a steady stream of water and said he wanted to do nothing but play his harpsichord, checkmate his lady at chess and feed the falcon on his wrist.

The woman who had worn the Mickey Mouse T-shirt earlier was now bedecked in the blue net dress decorated with silver paper fans. She sat beside me at dinner and complained that the fans were difficult to sit on. While I crunched away on a stick of celery, I saw Gilbert reach up into his mouth and pick a filling from one of his teeth off his tongue. He looked at it a bit cross-eyed and tried unsuccessfully to stick it back in.

Then everyone stood up and started to applaud. *La pièce montée* was being wheeled in on a dolly, a pastry pyramid made of glazed rum balls. Before he could cut it, Sean had to take a sword and slice the cork off a bottle of champagne, a ceremonial known as *sabré*. He held the bottle between his knees and sliced at the cork at an angle. He missed on the first two tries, but encouraged by the cheers of the crowd, he cracked it open on the third attempt.

Later I danced with him and he seemed stiff and hesitant. He steered us around the dance floor, his nose a prow, like a boy at his first prom dutifully dancing with his teacher. The dance ended and we heard another commotion—this time out in the meadow. Presently an outsized plywood horse was pushed into the theatre and an entire family emerged from its belly, all wearing togas. They looked around for whoever it was they had been sent to rescue.

Next I danced with Jean-Paul, who stared over my head and explained that the Trojan horse family had come over from London. Sean put down the sword he was using to cut the cake and made a beeline across the room to the youngest daughter, who had climbed from the horse in a daze, as if she didn't know where she was or how to handle herself.

By then nobody was bothering to play their roles. The new guests were hungry, having missed dinner, so they headed for the food. Sean, blinkered and transfixed, walked around the horse with this new girl, looking at the joints and touching the odd suggestions of a mane.

"*Tu dors, Kathleen?*" He came over to where I stood by the stable door.

"No, I thought I'd take a walk."

"*Veux-tu une petite lampe?*"

"Yes, please, it's pretty dark."

But Loesic had lent the flashlight to Gilbert, so Sean offered to come with me. We walked up a slope away from the castle where it was dark; soon the curtain of the fête was behind us and we could see the dark lining of the fabric. Wooden struts supported the cut-outs of dappled poplars; the laughter and music faded. Just past the turn in the road, we looked back over the scene on its sloping plinth. Sean sat down to take a stone out of his shoe. I sat down beside him, took off the heavy headdress and shook out my hair. He reached out to touch my arm. "There's a name in French for what you are, you know. You are *ma génitrice.*"

He went on to tell me that this was a difficult time for him, this summer, because after he finished his *bac* in science, he wanted to study film and communications. This summer he should try to find out something about his place in the world. Otherwise, why was he in his body? Why was he not a tree?

Then he wanted to get away. He wanted Christina, the girl in the white toga. He excused himself and later I found his crumpled gold tunic on the bathroom floor. I picked it up and hung it on a hanger. He had dropped a piece of gold gauze on the stairs leading up to the grenier, like a hanky, like a shoe.

The next morning Sean and Christina came strolling down the same path where I had seen him from the window the first day, between the chapel and the outbuildings. He said he was tired but happy. I wondered if he wasn't too tired to be happy. When I talked to Loesic later about him, she said, "Oh, Sean's in love again."

To my eyes he was in love the way Romeo was with Rosaline before he met Juliet. That afternoon in the kitchen I was getting ready to cook the carrots I had picked from the garden and Jean-Paul was reading the paper. Sean asked me if I was going to peel them before I cooked them.

"I don't when they're young and the skin is tender," I smiled.

He looked skeptical, then asked if I'd take the green stalks off or would I cook them too, ha ha. He picked up a dish towel and laughed at Poupon, his friend who'd just come in to sit down at the long table and who ate one yoghurt, then two yoghurts, three yoghurts, and Sean counted them, laughing because Poupon was still so bleary-eyed and it was four in the afternoon. His name, they said, came from his surname, Patoune, converted into the diminutive Poupon, like the inside of the cheeks on his face. Sean puffed his out at me and popped each one with his finger.

"And a little *nounours*, Kathleen, it's like a little bear."

"You've been to Germany quite a lot, haven't you?" I asked him. "Sophie told me you'd been to Germany."

"Sure."

"And New York too? I heard you went to New York?"

"New York isn't in Germany," he said, not looking at me but still laughing at Poupon.

The way his mouth turned down at the corners reminded me so much of Andrew that I felt thoroughly put down. His mouth—his wide sensuous mouth like his father's—curved quickly up and back again. He had just overheard me telling the others how worried I'd been making the phone call from London.

"You're a grown-up woman," he shouted. "Why should you be upset about making a phone call from London?"

As it happened, Poupon had been up longer than any of us knew, taking the decorations out of the theatre, he said, and piling them up in the kitchen, ready to be put away. On top of the pile was a large paper fish, and Sean pointedly asked Poupon why he had brought in that particular decoration when everyone knew it wasn't supposed to be taken down because that was the fish Jean-Paul had bought years ago, right after Niki phoned them from London. He had hung it on the door as they do in China when a man's wife is having a baby and he's hoping for a son. They left it hanging in place on the door when they decided to go to London. "Right, Maman?"

Loesic folded a quilt from the display she had arranged for the fête and taken down that afternoon. "I think he hung it up after we got back."

"No. It was before, Maman. Wasn't it, Papa?"

"Hmmm?" Jean-Paul looked up from his paper.

"The fish," Sean repeated, pointing to it. "You hung it in the doorway before I came to Paris."

"I don't remember. What I remember is the grilling we got at immigration."

"You had a bad time with the immigration?"

"We did, you know, Kathleen." Sean finished drying the last dish, stepped over to hold one end of the quilt for Loesic.

"You might have thought that everything went smoothly after we left your flat in London, but it wasn't what I'd call exactly relaxing having a baptism by air, I can tell you. I liked it, but . . ." He stepped up, slid his hand down the length of the quilt, picked up the bottom and stepped back as though performing a dance step in a minuet.

"You loved it. You slept the whole way." Loesic made the last fold and put the quilt aside.

"Yes, but Maman, when we got there, what about that?"

Loesic laughed, but Sean was in no mood to be dissuaded. He went to the end of the table and took Jean-Paul's chin in his hand. His father smiled obligingly, his cheeks moved higher up his face; the small red lines puffed as Sean turned his head from side to side.

"Look at this face, Kathleen, you see this face? Well, it didn't have its usual confidence, I can tell you, coming along in the airport with me in his arms." He turned back to his audience. He was trying to impress us as much as anything.

"The immigration officer looked accusingly at all three of our passports, consulted with a superior and then asked Jean-Paul to step into the interviewing room. He had to hand me over to Maman, who was obliged to wait on a chair like a new immigrant to her own country while the officials grilled her husband. But Papa had been used to that kind of difficulty during the war, so he stood up pretty well under the pressure. He was a hero, Kathleen, believe me. I mean, Papa, you were only sixteen when the war started, that's young."

"I thought we were talking about immigration." Jean-Paul turned back his newspaper.

No, the fact was that the Richters, Jean-Paul's parents . . . Sean now went over to curl up in the shabby brown chesterfield by the stove and insisted on telling me that way back then the senior Richter family been forced to leave their house in their village in Lorraine practically overnight when the war began. They could only take what they could carry. They were in a complete daze, as was everybody, because they'd all been told that the Maginot Line was impregnable and no one need worry about invasion, an assumption that turned out to be tragically wrong as Germany took over France in a little less than two months. It was August and everyone was on holiday. Since Paris was practically deserted, the enemy literally walked in. Sean was outraged by this every time he thought about it, and he thought about it all the time, he said. Especially since both France and Germany claimed Alsace and Lorraine. Thanks to the German conquest, Jean-Paul was taken into the German army.

Jean-Paul opened a bottle of wine. "I was young, it was all going to be an adventure, an escapade. I didn't know. None of us knew. They put me in a special division of the SS made up of men over six feet tall. I can tell you, it was a shock to our Catholic upbringing to learn that in time of war, notions of good and bad *n'existent plus*. The only reality that existed was if a person was killed or not killed."

"You were in the German army?"

"Yes, I was."

"But not for long, Kathleen." Sean touched my wrist. "You can imagine it was a terrible thing for a boy of that age to come up against the realization that he would have to escape, but that's what he had to do, didn't you, Papa? Anyway, he did escape and joined the French resistance, but then he was sent back into the German army as a spy. The first time he ever saw this region was when he landed in it by parachute in the terrible year of 1940."

"But do you know what it turned out to be at the immigration?" Jean-Paul interrupted Sean, laughing. "They were looking for a terrorist who looked like me—the same face and, I can't remember, was it the same name? Anyway, there were hours of bureaucratic nonsense I had to undergo to prove my identity. Hours."

"But we did get home," Loesic said.

"Yes, we did get home."

Later that evening, in the library, we looked through the family photo albums. Sean showed me all kinds of pic-

tures, including a snapshot of a particular cat they had
had when he was a baby. They'd only been back from
London a short time, he said, when he and Maman were
down in the basement of their apartment building looking
through their storeroom for some drawings by the painter
and designer of *Vogue* covers who had lived there before
them, a man by the name of Lepape. Maman had found
much better drawings in the basement than any of the
Vogue covers he'd been famous for. One day they were
down there looking for more, but instead of the trunks
full of drawings they'd hoped to find, they found a cat
that jumped down off a ledge and scratched Maman with
its claws. No cat had ever scratched Maman before—
Maman liked cats—but unfortunately the scratch became
infected and this *griffure de chat* made her so sick she
couldn't look after Sean properly, and so they were forced
to hire *une fille au pair*. This fille au pair called Dorothée,
from Bavaria, was very nice, but the problem turned out
to be that Jean-Paul had arrived at that tender age in his
forties when a man can get caught in the snare of wondering whether he could reach out and turn the face of an au
pair around to kiss her, and if she would open her mouth
to him when he did that. Every time he looked at
Dorothée he grew dizzy with this possibility—there she
was on every side of him all over the apartment—and
although Dorothée respected Maman—everybody re-
spects Maman, Sean said—and she didn't want to upset
the equilibrium of the family, she was in a terrible position "because Papa is irresistible," Sean said, laughing.
You can't blame Dorothée. No, really, Kathleen, you can't
blame Dorothée. Anyway, what with all this going on,
Maman decided to take him on a visit to Brittany to see

her relatives and see if she could let time decant this matter of Dorothée. While they were in Brittany, they had gone to see the dolmens de Carnac. Nobody ever did know what those stones were for. In the picture he showed me, they looked like women in shawls, walking away in a dusty line. Further into the groupings—the *menhirs*, he called them—he was hiding behind one, crouched down by another playing hide-and-seek with the photographer. Sean pulled another leather-bound album off the shelf.

"Maman sent you that picture? I wonder why she sent you that one? I'm trying to tell you about my double life, Kathleen. Ma vie à *double fond*. You know, like a spy who has a suitcase with two compartments?"

The windows in the library were tall, opening out across the field to distant poplars and the faraway hills almost transparent in the haze. I kept wanting to stop him turning the pages, take the photos out, arrange and rearrange them in different combinations. Stop, I wanted to say, you're going too fast. That's my baby.

But he kept flipping through the plastic-bound pages of the album, finally stopping at another picture of himself running through the stone figures. He told me Loesic always remembered his first sentence. He had run around in his black wool sweater among the dolmens of Carnac until his legs gave out, then flopped in her lap. "*Assez de cailloux, Maman*. I've had it with these pebbles."

Anyway, Sean continued, it wasn't long before Dorothée returned to Bavaria, but when Sean and Loesic got back to Paris, they found that Jean-Paul had lost his sense of humour and Maman wanted to find a new project that would help solidify the family. So, here's where they first started to have picnics at Pruniers; the first snapshot of it was nothing more than a ruin with the stones from the roof fallen into the centre pit. There they are sitting on the ground with a checkered tablecloth and a picnic basket. I hardly had time to look at that page before he was on to the next. Each time they visited, the place seemed more overgrown. The turf had hooped into a mass of brambles so that what was left of the old fortress and outbuildings seemed to be collapsing in slow motion. The roof had crumbled away stone by stone, and the chapel and stables and granges were in ruins. More and more stones fell into the centre. The structure was like the kind of castles children draw, oversimplified square buildings with towers in each corner and one tower that no one ever went into except the keeper of the keys.

Every time they visited, the idea of restoring the place seemed both more impossible and more compelling. They inveigled an architect friend who had studied mediaeval structures to have a look, and he told them to forget it; the price they would get for selling Bouchauds would only be enough to pay for the restoration of the roof.

But Loesic had decided that the family needed those walls, and that sense of history, because eventually she was going to tell Sean that his *génitrice* had given him to them because she loved him and, logically, there would be nothing to prevent him from concluding that the strength of his parents' love was no guarantee he would not lose his place with them. The castle would provide that extra strength he needed for security.

"Really?"

"Yes, that's what she thought."

Even the retired French army general who owned the

place tried to discourage them, but Maman had made up her mind and that was that. Then, when they got the estimate for fixing the roof and knew they wouldn't have enough money to make the down payment, the general gave them a mortgage. They were kept pretty busy as they cleared and cleared, because at the time there was nothing down there on the inside where all the rooms were now. There was only a hole.

After we finished looking at the photographs, we went back to the kitchen. Sean went into the back bedroom off the kitchen to call Christina, who had left for Paris with her parents on the morning train. He came back in and announced that he was going to London. To visit Christina.

"*Je vais à Londres,*" he said, as if nothing were going to stand in his way.

"He used to be so placid when he was little," Loesic murmured.

"What are your plans, Kathleen?"

"I'm going back to Vancouver on the third."

"Good, I'm going to Paris tomorrow. Do you want to come with me?"

I looked at Loesic. She nodded.

"That'd be really nice."

Jean-Paul turned to him. "You're not going to get any money to spend on clothes in London, Sean."

"Why not? Clothes are much cheaper in London, aren't they, Kathleen?"

"I don't know. I haven't shopped there for a long time."

That night Loesic and I had a talk. We were in the bathroom; she was putting away the make-up and the

rosettes. I sat on the counter by the sink where the ironing board had been. She told me she was no longer
happy in Paris; there were no surprises for her there
any more. She looked forward to their retirement so
they could spend more time at Pruniers. She said she
had tried to bring Sean up to be self-sufficient, but it
was difficult to get him to look after his clothes or cook
when his father didn't do those things. Theirs had been
a traditional marriage. Jean-Paul was the breadwinner,
she ran the home.

"You've done an incredible job."

"You have too."

Dear Mom: I long for the day when we will be able
to show Sean around our property at the creek. Do
you think such a day will come?

"Would it be all right with you and Jean-Paul if Sean
came out to Canada for a visit one day? Just for a couple
of weeks? Sophie and I would really like to show him
around."

"*Bien sûr.*"

We exchanged that same level look, the look of col-
leagues, that had passed between us years ago in the
kitchen at Bennington Gardens. It said we knew that the
situation would be confusing for him, that his life would
be complicated.

The next day when Sean and I were ready to leave,
Jean-Paul and Loesic stood in front of the chateau as the
taxi pulled up, the established couple in front of their
place of residence. I was fighting tears at leaving them,
but Sean was impatient. "Come on, Kathleen. Let's go,"

he said from the back seat as he leaned over the front seat to shove the door open.

"*A bientôt*," I said as each of them bent in the front window and we kissed.

In the train, Sean and Poupon and the others who were coming to Paris sprawled on the luggage on the platform between the cars. An old man took out bits of cheese wrapped in wax paper held together with an elastic band, a tobacco pouch and his wallet, and laid them all out on his lap. Then he carefully wrapped them all up again. Sean found the last seat for me and put my bag on the overhead rack. I couldn't believe that I had him all to myself for two whole days.

The Paris apartment seemed run-down and neglected, and the bed I was to sleep in stood where the bentwood cradle had glowed in my mind for so many years. There were more baby pictures of him on the wall that I could stare at for as long as I wanted. Sean's other girl friend was coming over. She didn't know about Christina yet.

"What are you going to do?"

"*On verra.*"

"Well, when you go to London, you were born in a hospital called St. Mary's in Paddington if you want to have a look at it."

"Sure."

He didn't seem interested. He had a one-track mind now, a track leading straight to Christina, the perfect English schoolgirl with her Christopher Robin haircut and pleated skirt. Back outside, Pigalle was tough and flattened with the smell of predatory lust. Sean walked around the district like a street kid, moving through the streets swiftly as if he knew every corner and turn in the maze.

THREE

6

The weather was hot when I got home, baking down in an Indian summer heat. The garden had stood up well. Kim, my downstairs neighbour and landlady, had been watering and eating from it. Lots of mail. School clothes and books to pick up, child support cheques to flag down, cleaning, washing, friends of the kids calling to find out where they were. Mother asked perfunctorily if I'd had a nice time, and wanted to know when Luke was getting back and would he be coming for dinner Wednesday nights or Thursday nights? A new crop of lettuce to put in so we would have greens in October. Classes to prepare. Normal life.

Sophie was waiting for me, anxious to sort out how things now stood with the Richters. She sat on the swing in the backyard, dragging her legs back and forth on the ground while I got caught up in the garden. The mountains were undeniably blue and present and it was good to breathe fresh air again after the long plane ride. Luke was coming in later that day and everything would get back to a regular routine.

"I have to tell you, Mom, Dad says he's going back to London. I wrote to him about seeing him but he wrote back about his schedule with this band he's in in Louisiana and didn't even mention our plans. What am I supposed to make of this? It's like a newsletter."

She'd gone down to visit Andrew a couple of summers ago—I'd had trouble locating him but she was determined to spend some time with him. That was good; she had to know who her father was if only to help her sort out her relationships with men. I didn't know how or why he'd ended up in Louisiana but, when she got there, he bought her a black cowboy shirt so she could go around with his band. She'd practically lived in it.

"Are you going to talk to him about Sean or what? I can't believe my brother's coming here. You mean he's going to get off a plane and walk down the tarmac, just like that?" Before I'd left Paris, Sean and I had worked out a plan. He would extend his trip to London on to Vancouver so that he could see where we lived. He'd been excited about the idea. I saw him look across the room at an imaginary horizon. I'm coming there, he'd said.

"Looks like it."

"We'd better get thinking about food. He'll be wanting pancakes. He had pancakes in New York and thought they were the greatest thing since sliced bread."

"The French don't have sliced bread, they have baguettes."

"Right, Mother. Listen, did you talk to Sean about Andrew or what?"

"Yes, I did."

Years earlier, when Sean was very young, I had told Andrew that I was certain Sean was his son, but he'd never asked me for an address, let alone tried to get in touch. I'd told Sophie about that too. I didn't want her getting her expectations up. Even so, the notion of taking the situation out, examining it and putting it away again didn't satisfy her either. It seemed to satisfy her even less now that I'd been over there. Perhaps she hoped I would bring back the missing piece of the jigsaw. But perhaps if I began taking the responsibility of Pruniers off her shoulders and replacing her presence there with mine, it would give her some relief and a sense of balance. Normalize it. Tell her matter-of-factly the daily things that had happened.

I lifted stems and leaves, looking for some zucchini that weren't too overgrown. The soil was heavy and packed down tightly under my gum boots as I pulled out the last of the beets. The turnips would be okay for a while, their purple bulbs edging up over the soil. I didn't want to see Sophie spending her life travelling around the world trying to gather up her family.

"When was it you and Sean talked about Andrew?"

"One morning when we were sitting at that round tin table."

"The one they drag out every time the sun comes out?"

"I think so."

"Overlooking the meadow where they play soccer?"

"That's it. At first I thought I shouldn't because of Jean-Paul and Loesic, but they . . . Well, whenever Gilbert was near to translate, Jean-Paul would be there too, putting chairs under all three of us. Talk, he would say, talk. He didn't push it that hard but there was real pressure in their voices, so I thought . . ."

Sophie stopped the swing and leaned forward. "That he should have the basic information, you mean?"

"Yes."

And it wasn't just when Gilbert was around with Sean and me on those final sunny afternoons, either; he helped all of us. Through Gilbert, Loesic and Jean-Paul told me hesitantly how awkward it had been for them having nothing substantial to go on all these years. We agreed that there just isn't any language to cope with the problems of adoption, let alone any established guidelines for dealing with a situation that is far more common than is generally acknowledged. We laughed when we realized that we'd been telling Sean and Sophie exactly the same story at the same time. I couldn't help wondering whether we hadn't used what the adoption experts call the magical explanation ("It was all meant to be") with Sean in order to avoid facing the reality of adoption.

"What I'm saying, Soph, is that when we were talking there by the soccer field I tried to think of things that would help fill in the gaps for him. Like when your dad was in Holiday Theatre practising dance steps." Holiday Theatre was a touring company for children that Andrew had joined for a while before we went to England. It travelled around the province taking the old gold rush route up through the Cariboo and the Chilcotin.

I pulled up a broccoli, shook off the roots and tossed it in a straw basket. I'd planted bush beans between a bunch of planks I'd put down for paths but they were mildewed and had turned black; they were past their season anyway. The robins were working over the mountain ash berries and the sumac, getting ready to fly to Mexico.

"When?"

"Well, when he was trying to get right movements for

the fox in *Pinocchio*, or maybe it was for the Jester role in . . . what play was it now?"

"It doesn't matter."

"I think it was the Jester role. Anyway, he had to jump up and put his toe to his calf in mid-air and he couldn't get the jump right. We were up in one of the rooms above the old auditorium. I was trying to help, and smiled once when he did it wrong, gently I thought, I didn't mean to . . . But he was angry and said, just because *I* could do it . . . He's a fine actor, your dad." How many times had I said that? "Here, put these cucumbers in the basket."

"You said all that in English?"

"No, just that he had . . . these parts."

"What did Sean do?" She dropped her hands between her knees, anchoring the swing. The sunflowers had grown up over the fence and were ready to be hung for birdseed. Too much to do. Already, the trip seemed like a dream, not that it had seemed like anything else when I was actually there. I stood up to tie my scarf tighter against a slight wind that had come up.

"He listened but he had one eye on . . . well, we were outside so there wasn't a door. But it was Christina. He didn't want to let her out of his sight. Another time"—I had to smile—"I told him if he was coming to visit I'd be sure to have an iron handy, because he irons his clothes all the time. He just kept his head down and went on with his ironing. There was one picture on the wall in the room where I slept when he's maybe two, and I could tell he had the same slightly moist skin you did that smelled like new potatoes."

"Potatoes?"

"New potatoes."

"Did you notice how big his vaccination mark is?"

"No."

"Well, it's big."

I handed her some baskets to take into the basement; it was time to drive out to the airport to pick up Luke. She sat over against the car door, looking out the window. At the corner I turned off our street with its small white bungalows and clipped lawns. One house had stained glass, another a spectacular azalea garden and another endless rococo aluminum trim and plastic fountains. Sophie claimed the owners had won the prize for the ugliest house on the block and then used the prize money to fix it up.

She seemed confused. I kept thinking I'd gone about things all wrong. Maybe we should have used a different explanation right from the beginning, one that was more realistic, compelling and enduring, as they say. Maybe acknowledging a mutual sense of deprivation would have been a better approach for all of us right from the start. Telling Sophie that she and I had a loss in common might have given us a more substantial bond. Such an explanation would certainly be a more convincing reason for an adopted child to believe in his or her connection with the foster family than making too much of the "magical explanation," which had left Sophie in such an unprotected position. The Richters had clearly managed to sustain an appreciation of Sean's beginnings and may well have sympathized with the fact that, just as he had been deprived of his natural roots without consent, so Loesic had been deprived of giving birth. Her own sense of deprivation might have helped her understand how it would have felt for him to sustain his loss.

Still, everything always looks different when you look

back at where you've been from a new vantage point. Sometimes when I was thinking about the past and looking at Sean, he avoided my eyes, looking to the side as if wondering who I was looking for. I could see now that Sophie's appearance in his world must have been threatening.

But, on the other hand, he had told me he would never forget meeting Sophie for the first time when she'd come to them in Paris. They'd both been really shy because they didn't speak the same language, and he stood over to one side and she stood over to the other and they both kept darting looks at each other. Once, he remembered, he lifted a low hanging branch for her to swim under when they were in the river. He would pass her more bread and fruit and more of any of the dishes on the table he could get his hands on. Once, when he walked by her where she was lying in a deck chair with a shirt over her face, he'd lifted it up and peered inside to tease her. After she left, he always had to have a picture of her in his room in Paris, he said.

Sophie wanted to stop at Baskin-Robbins for ice cream; she regresses when she's stressed. She got a strawberry ripple cone and that cheered her up. The river ran grey and slow as we crossed the bridge. All kinds of birds lined the shores, and masses of starlings swayed on the wires overhead, chippering away.

I'd often wondered, after I'd told Luke about Sean, if Luke ever worried that I would abandon him. Always, at the end of summer, when he arrived back on the west coast, he needed to have his sense of security stroked. It always took a while for him to adjust to the fact, for instance, that he couldn't reach in the fridge, pull out a

155

quart of milk and drink the whole thing when he came in from playing. It was hard enough that I'd been married twice and that'd he had to travel back and forth across the continent to see both his father and me. I hoped my trip wouldn't create more problems than it solved.

"What else happened?" Sophie asked.

I glanced over at her. "Well, let's see. I thought people must put in for food, but decided maybe it would be better for me to buy something and help with the cooking."

"They didn't let me pay for any food when I was there," Sophie said. "So I cooked when Loesic went to Pruniers."

"You had the money."

"I know."

"Curries, right? You said."

"Right."

"Well, I thought lamb."

"But it was summer. It wouldn't be in season."

"It wasn't, but I couldn't think what else and they had some in the freezer in the village. It's pretty hard to go wrong with a leg of lamb. You know how I like to do what I'm sure of when it's for company. Anyway, I'd seen mint growing in the yard in the corner by the west tower. I thought they might like to try that, maybe they'd never had mint sauce with lamb." We were close to the airport now. A plane flew low, coming in for a landing. I looked for a parking space.

"Did they like it?"

"Sure they liked it. So anyway, I said I'd cook *de l'agneau*, and everyone laughed at the way I pronounced it."

"*De l'agneau.*"

"That's what I said."

"No, you didn't, you said *lagnew*." I found a place, squeezed in.

"Well, anyway. Let's see, what else? You know when you're going into the village?" I put the car in park and stayed sitting in the driver's seat. "Well, the day after the fête we went to return the trays Loesic had borrowed for the banquet. She was standing there by the car and, before she got in, she bent the windshield wipers straight out, you know the way you do when you're cleaning the windshield, and then turned them on"—I wagged my hand back and forth—"and left them like that while we drove. Like antennae. I was in the back seat and she and Sean just drove along not making any comment with the wipers swinging back and forth in front of the windshield all the way there and back. It was really funny. He was learning to drive, and even when they stopped and changed places, she left them flapping. She helped herself to a *frite* and an apricot when we returned the trays, but the storekeeper seemed used to that, I guess she's a good customer."

"She is. Did Sean drive there or back?"

"Uh, back."

"Has he got his licence yet?"

"I'm not sure."

We got out, headed for the arrivals section and peered up at the monitor showing the incoming passengers going through customs, but none of the grey figures coming around the corner was Luke. We finally asked the people coming out if this was the flight from Seattle; it was. I started to worry. Finally a customs officer came out and led us back inside. There was Luke, stocky, brown and tired, with his wind-surfer pulled up to the customs booth like a beached whale.

"Hi, Mom."

"Hi, honey. What's all this?"

He looked exhausted. I put my arm around him and he leaned against me. His hair smelled of dry salt. The customs officer wanted to know the value of the goods he was bringing back and Luke had rattled off random amounts, bragging, probably. "Oh, the wind-surfer's worth about a thousand, I guess. And the harness and the mast another five hundred."

The customs officer handed me a bill for $310.

"What's this?"

"Customs duty. These are the figures we've added up. Based on the goods your son is bringing back."

"But I don't know anything about this. He's been visiting his father in the States."

"Well, that's the charge and you'll have to pay it or we'll have to confiscate the equipment."

Luke burst into tears. "Luke, darling, don't worry, we'll figure this out. Look, officer, this is obviously secondhand stuff. It just doesn't make sense. It's not worth more than two or three hundred dollars."

There was no one else in the customs room; we could hear the hum of the fluorescent lights, and the near-empty baggage carousels circled endlessly, a couple of forlorn suitcases disappearing and reappearing on the belt. The customs people were tired and irritable. "But that's not what the lad is saying. Are you sure you don't have a sales slip? Did your dad buy these from a store or a private seller or what?"

"A private seller."

"Then a receipt wouldn't do us any good anyway. He could have made out a sales slip for any old amount." He turned his attention to stamping some slips, part of his closing-up routine.

"My son must have been thinking of these items new. The thing's covered in scratches and dents. There's no way it's worth a thousand dollars."

Eventually we compromised. They would phone a sporting goods store in the morning and get an estimate on secondhand wind-surfing equipment, and we'd take it from there. We had to leave the board with them. Luke was upset during the ride home and only cheered up when he began talking about wind-surfing. Last year it had been break dancing. Sophie was a child who seemed to carry her world around with her, but Luke was always right out there in the middle of wherever he was, reacting spontaneously to whatever was going on. As soon as we got home, he rushed off into the back lane, calling on his friends to set up the street hockey net.

I had bought fresh pasta at the market and made pesto for supper with the last of the basil from the garden. Luke looked at what I was doing and said, "At Dad's they have a machine and make their own pasta. Just before they cook it."

"They do, do they?"

He asked about my trip, but he was not nearly as interested in hearing about his imaginary brother as he was in checking in with his friends.

"So then what happened?" Sophie was not going to let go of any of this. She couldn't get enough. She had decided to stay the night and sat at the kitchen table, her legs pulled up, knees under her chin. We put water on for tea and sat across from each other looking down at the square-cut backyards along the block. The neighbour's magnolia tree had folded up for the season and the forsythia no longer raged in the lane. I took the mugs down from the rough wood kitchen shelves. Luke's father was the love of my life—there was no denying that, and sometimes I thought that Luke's grandfather's ghost lived under the house where we had gone at the time of our first meeting and where Luke spent part of every summer. His grandfather had built the house where I fell so desperately in love that I barely got out of the relationship alive, fleeing to my own country like a refugee.

I pulled myself back. "Where was I?"

"You were in the kitchen making lamb."

"Oh, right. Well, it was fine. I think it was after dinner that night—or was it the morning after the fête?—anyway, somewhere in there the conversation got around to the time when Sean was born and they were bringing him back from London. God, I hope it's okay tomorrow, I really can't afford to pay three hundred bucks for that wind-surfer."

"Don't worry, it'll be okay."

I poured our tea. "Apparently—did you hear about this? How Jean-Paul was interrogated when they got to the airport in Paris and Loesic had to sit with Sean outside the cubicle for hours worrying about what was going on?"

"They thought my dad had sent out an alert?"

"Oh, Sophie, maybe they did think that. Maybe they did."

We were both quiet for a moment searching each other's faces across the table. "Go on, please, Mom."

I told her about how, on the same night we were talking about the immigration problem, everyone got into an argument about whether Loesic had ever been scratched by a cat before the time that one had attacked her in *les caves* when she got so sick. "I don't even know how it came up or why everyone was so worked up, but one contingent at the dinner table swore up and down that she was wrong, saying that she did know she was allergic to cats because the doctor had said so way back when they were all living in l'Hôtel Liberty near la Place Monge and that it had definitely been soon after the liberation because Jean-Paul had just started his business repairing stained glass windows. Then they began to argue about whether the people who left Paris during the occupation and only came back when the Germans were gone had in some way collaborated . . ."

"Mom, it was worse than that. People were turning in suspected collaborators and half the Resistance was breaking off into factions." She was doing her nails, darting glances up at me.

"Right. Well, anyway, someone else said—you know how they talk. It's like no one can make a move without consulting everyone else. No, it most definitely had been in l'Hôtel Liberty near la Place Monge and that person knew there had been a cat there because they didn't have a telephone and climbing all those stairs took too much time, so they used to send messages across the courtyard by bow and arrow. I couldn't figure out what any of this had to do with having a cat, but in the end, it didn't really seem to be an argument about whether Loesic had been scratched by a cat before or not. I got the feeling that the argument was about something else altogether."

"Do you know what it was about?"

"Not really."

"It was about Dorothée."

"Oh, you know about that?"

"Oh, sure."

"Yeah, well," I sighed. "I guess it wasn't all peaches and cream for them either. It seems like Loesic didn't have such an easy time of it. Nothing could feel worse, when you've just had a baby and you feel unattractive and exhausted, and that's the time your husband picks to have an affair."

"But, Mom . . ."

"No, really, I have to hand it to her, how she managed to divert everyone's attention by getting them thinking about restoring Pruniers and all the rest of it."

"But, Mom, you had the baby, not Loesic."

"Oh, good grief, Sophie, what am I thinking about?"

"Kathleen, I'm calling you from London."

"Where are you in London?"

"I don't know. In a phone booth somewhere."

"Well, just get on the plane and come, okay? We can hardly wait."

A scrim of mist hung over the mountains and the first leaves had begun to turn. In the early fall, the deciduous trees finally get their moment and stand out in fiery red or bright yellow for a few short days against the pine and fir. I tripped over the empty can of paint on my way out to get another can to finish painting the guest room for Sean. A twist of smoke clouds rose from behind the nearest blue hill. The ocean was navy green. Sophie got another card from Andrew. *Events have conspired to keep us in London.* She panicked. What if Sean and Andrew passed each other on the street? They were both going to be there at the same time. I said it probably wouldn't happen; it's the sort of thing you imagine happening but usually doesn't. She said no, it's the sort of thing that usually *does.*

Luke had invented a new game with the spaghetti server and a golf ball that he bounced down the stairs, and no one could go up or down while he was playing it without giving the password.

"Luke, for heaven's sake, let me by. I've got to go shopping. I don't know the password." It didn't matter that I had painted the floor in his room while he was away; to his mind, I should have painted his room, too, if I was going to paint the spare room for Sean.

On the day of his brother's arrival, Luke's bike was leaning up against the wall inside the front door, with the pea net I'd left on the swing set all twisted up in the spokes. First he wasn't going to come to the airport with us, then he was, then he wasn't. Finally, he decided to play hockey in the lane and wait for us.

We were late. I gave a toot on the horn, and Sophie dashed out of the house in black velvet pants and her leopard-skin coat, passed her lipstick, compact and eyebrow pencil through the car window and asked me to hold them for her. She took her bearings from a quick glance at the house and mountains, reached around inside the front door to unlock the back, climbed in and stretched out on the back seat. We might have to stop, she said. She might have to be sick. She could stay here, wait at home. Oh, no, she had to come.

When we got to the airport, she forgot to ask me for her make-up; instead, she stood beside the car looking pale. She pressed anxiously at her cheek as we walked through the parking lot. The sky was bright and glaring.

"Do you know what they said to me when I was over there, Mom? They said that because I didn't make a fuss over my clothes or comb my hair before I went out that I was afraid to be a woman, that's what they said." She was having trouble keeping up with me although normally she took longer strides than I did.

"They had no idea then, did they?" I checked the arrival time on the telegram and hoped we weren't late.

"They said it was too bad I wasn't staying any longer because then we could talk about my psychological problems. I thought I was there to talk about *his* psychological problems. I guess that business about my baseball cap really worried him. He just didn't get it that I was wearing it to ward off street wolves."

"It's okay, Soph. It's going to be okay." I took her hand.

No lengthy wait in the terminal this time. Within minutes, there he was, coming straight through the gates grinning. He looked tired but pleased to be here; it was the middle of the night his time. I had booked his flight so he would pass over the Rockies in the daylight and see the spectacular jagged line stretching to the North Pole. As we stood there, a woman in a striped dress trailed her suitcase past us. Sean waved to her distractedly; perhaps she'd been his seat-mate. It was great to see him; it was even better to hold him.

"Did you have any problems with the customs or immigration people, Sean?"

"*Non. Pas de problèmes.*"

"Good. Let's go home."

As we were getting organized, he looked closely at Sophie, as if trying to see through her skin to the shape of her white bones.

"Did you see the Rockies? Aren't they amazing?" The minute I saw him I felt in Loesic and Jean-Paul's debt. Loesic must have been feeling the same physical pull as I did in all my cells when Luke was away from me.

"Sure, I saw the Rockies. Here, I'll take that, it's too heavy for you, Kathleen. It's really heavy."

"I like your purse."

"Thanks. It's Jean-Paul's."

"How is Jean-Paul?"

"Much better." He had suffered a slight stroke about a month before and had been in hospital. I had been writing and calling but hadn't received the latest news.

"That's good."

At home we rounded the bannister and filed up the stairs. The year before, about this time, the three of us painted the whole apartment grey with white trim. I was glad it looked nice now. Luke was waiting at the top of the stairs smiling his good-natured smile. He reached down for Sean's bag. "Hi, Sean."

"*Salut, Luke.*"

I was so happy to have them all together; they could have asked me to sweep a parking lot and I'd have been only too glad. A fresh clean wind blew through the house and with it the faint smell of sweet peas. Everything seemed clean and bright and fresh. Sean sat down on the yellow couch and began bringing out presents. For Luke, a slim white volume called *Sources d'Amitié*. Luke politely did not mention that he wouldn't be able to understand it.

A handsome book of paintings from the Louvre—"You have Maman to thank for that"—and three invitations to next year's fête. This one would be a seventeenth-century affair complete with powdered wigs and hoop-skirted dresses. Next he went off to explore the apartment, shouldering himself in and out of the white bay-windowed angles, trying them on like outsized coats and shrugging them off again. The windows were all open. He liked the rooms and nodded his approval as if he had expected these windows and hardwood floors and piles of books and plants to be arranged just as they were. Sophie was cheered by his clear delight in our home. As I went to make some lemonade I heard him from the guest room at the top of the house. He called down. "Is this where I'm going to sleep?"

"Yes."

"Good."

He came back down. "The apartment is fine, *c'est très beau.*" He said it reminded him of the atmosphere at Bouchauds. I wondered how he could remember; he was only three years old when they sold Bouchauds.

I had invited some friends for a potluck supper: Kim, my landlady, Haida from down the street, my friend Donna and Sophie's new boyfriend, Tim. Haida had waved from her yard as we got back from the airport. She had been cutting her grass, pushing her old hand lawn mower up and down under her shady walnut tree, looking wonderful with her close-cropped hair and white lawn dress.

This was joy then, the lightness that had suddenly come into the house. Sean found the bottle of chilled wine in the fridge without having to ask and carried the glasses to the coffee table in the living room, waving them upside down by the stems. As we waited for people to arrive, Sophie stretched out on the sofa, Sean seated on the arm above her. She listened and smiled; it was where she wanted to be. Her carefully painted toenails reached out to rest on my knee at one end and she slipped her hand into Sean's at the other. Luke stood in the doorway with a bowl of chili and some salad.

"Aren't you going to wait for the sushi, love?"

"Raw fish, gross."

We laughed with him. The deeper shadows moved across the city as dusk fell and the lights came on. The starlings set up their usual racket on the telephone wires. "The thing is, Kathleen, when you have a dream and don't pay attention to it, it's like getting a letter and not opening it, don't you think?" He said this carefully in English, as if he'd rehearsed it.

"Yes."

"Are you interested in psychology?"

"Yes."

"Shake hands." We reached across Sophie, whose toes nestled further into my knees. Luke looked up from where he stood by the door. "You ever done any windsurfing, Sean?" We'd recovered the board at an even hundred, far too much by my estimate.

"No, I haven't, but it looks great."

"Want to try?"

"You bet."

He smiled at Luke, then stretched his eyes out across the inlet as if trying to commit one further peak to memory. Then suddenly he announced that he really wanted to talk to me about Salome. So many names had come up, so many people he wanted me to know, I thought at first this was some girl I had met at Pruniers.

"Who?"

"Salome. The one who danced for Herod."

"Oh, her."

Difficult as it was while sitting on a sofa arm, he managed to cross one leg over the other and press on in English. Whereas I'd mostly struggled in French at Pruniers, he was initiating English here. His English was far better than my French. "The thing is, Kathleen, I'm writing a film script about her. It all happens in the sixties. There's a man who meets this girl and he keeps asking her to try this drug or that and, well, she does . . ." He stood up, went over to the window. "And she dies. He tries to forget that he encouraged or forced her, which is wrong, but he has to pretend that he didn't so he doesn't have to face the guilt."

He seemed to be addressing the window, standing a few inches away from it, keeping the conversation going to give the quieter part of himself time to arrive.

"But then one day . . ." The dog wandered in and heaved himself under the coffee table. "He's in a gallery and he turns a corner and sees a painting called *Salome* and the woman holding the head has the same face as the girl he killed. But instead of holding the head of John the Baptist, she has the hair of another woman hooked in her fingers and the look on her face is one of guilty pleasure."

"The head's face?"

"No, the face of Salome."

"What happened to the rest of her body?"

"I don't know. So what do you think of it?"

The dog twitched in his sleep. Luke thought he'd go

and watch "Star Trek." The dog woke up and followed Luke into his room.

"Maybe what he does with the suppressed guilt might be the fuel for the story, is that a possibility?" I said this without really thinking about it. My mind was on dinner.

"Maybe."

"You have a ways to go on it, do you?"

"Yes."

"There's a typewriter up in your room. It's on the old desk in there and the blue room is quiet."

"Good."

A few minutes later, Kim arrived wearing a purple silk dress hand-stamped in orange butterflies and carrying platters of fresh tuna and seaweed. She was born in a village near Kyoto and learned to make sushi at her mother's knee. Our house had been raised up off its foundations to make room for a basement apartment. The house tilted, and water from the faucet ran down the counter towards the door instead of into the sink. Kim collected a substantial rent each month for the four apartments, but she was always having to fix something or other. She welcomed Sean with an outstretched arm and we all stood around admiring the evening.

"Hi up there. I'm coming up." Haida appeared with a jug of hot sake. Sophie began to regale her with stories about the horrors of tanning. Haida had run into Sophie with her friends at Kits Beach the day before, lying on blankets under the sun all done up in wide hats with scarfs and long dresses.

"People were very offended," said Sophie. Haida laughed; she'd noticed, she said. She peered at Sean over the top of her half-glasses. "Hello, you must be Sean."

At last my friends were coming to the hospital to see my baby. We pulled a couple of low coffee tables together. Donna arrived with a red comb in her hair, turquoise running shoes and a bouquet of alstroemaria. She had excellent lines at the corners of her mouth and lived among pastel ceramics in the back of the Hawks Street Reading Room.

Sean sprawled on the floor on some cushions and demonstrated to Sophie all the different ways you could kiss a woman's hand and what each variation meant. We all watched, fascinated. Sophie's new boyfriend, Tim, had red curls and a Pre-Raphaelite face; for his band's next gig, they planned to create a hospital emergency room and wear nurses' uniforms with winged caps. She had bought Tim a nylon nurse's uniform—tomorrow they had to find wigs. The white dress smelled of stale cigarette smoke from being in Value Village for too long. Sophie hung it on the porch to air out.

After the meal, Haida and Donna and Kim and I got up from the pillows and retired to the kitchen table for coffee while the young people stayed in the living room. All but Sean, who joined us, his Burberry trench coat draped over his shoulders. He turned a chair backward, sat down and rested his head on his elbow bent along the chair back. He then said that he and Sophie and Tim and some of their friends were going off to a club.

"That's fine," said Haida. "Clean your teeth and be back by midnight."

Her funny style of pretending to be yet another mother made him decide he was in no hurry after all, and he settled into our conversation, giving himself over to it as he did when he looked at a photograph or a book. Haida, who is a film editor, promised to take him down to the National Film Board and show him around. I felt gratefully relieved, as I had when we had moved into this neighbourhood and Luke started making friends.

Sean thought that, after all, maybe it was too late for him to go to this club; he said he was afraid that if he left he'd miss something. After listening to us talk for a while, he mentioned that what he liked to listen to was the innuendo, the nervous vibration of the sound of the language under the language. He'd been like that since he was a baby, he said, hearing the sound heavings of people talking before he really understood their words.

Luke told me when I went in to say good night that he had felt both funny and at ease about meeting Sean; it reminded him of the time he had seen an actor from a TV show on the street and thought he knew him but knew he didn't.

"Coming up the stairs with your face," he said, "there was this Frenchman smelling like perfume and the plane and like he needed a shower. I liked the way his hand felt and wondered how mine felt to him." Other than that, he'd lost the socks to his soccer uniform and did I know where they were? I sat with him a little longer than usual until he settled down.

The dog had to be walked, so after the others left—no, he wasn't ready for bed yet—Sean and I went out into the velvet evening. We passed all the sleeping stucco bungalows, turned the corner of the block and headed back down the lane. He liked my friends, he said. Kim was so nice and Haida was unique and Donna was beautiful and more reserved. Couldn't argue with that. Back home, he sat down on the kitchen table. Whatever I might have had in mind, he had his own agenda.

"I've been meaning to ask you, Kathleen, what time of day was I born?"

"About noon. Early afternoon." I hung up the leash.

"Didn't you write down the exact time?"

"I didn't, no."

"It's important, you know. For astrology."

"It was between twelve-thirty and two, isn't that good enough?"

"Not really. I always thought it was late at night or early morning, about dawn."

"Do you want it to have been?"

"It doesn't matter."

He was nearly falling down from exhaustion but kept finding other things to bring up with me. How long had I lived there? Had I gone to school as a child near there? He found it hard to put his meaning into words but at the same time couldn't stop trying.

"What about some sleep now, love? We have two whole weeks to talk. I love you, Sean."

His eyes opened wide. "I love you, too, Kathleen."

Whatever it was, he couldn't seem to give it up. He remained sitting there, legs crossed like a garden statue of a leprechaun. I put my arm around him and, at last, he slowly uncrossed his legs and made his way up to the blue room where the window was open and his bed was waiting.

In the morning, I found Luke sitting on his mussed-up bed reading the Saturday comics. The first autumn fog had rolled in. A bunch of kids were playing lacrosse in the middle of the street and I wondered how they could see either the ball or the net.

"Those kids are up pretty early," I said.

Normally he'd be out there with them, but that day he followed me into the kitchen, padding across the floor in his unmatched socks and picking at the threads in his terry-cloth dressing gown. Sean, in a spotless white piqué robe, was stirring bran into boiling water.

"What are you doing, kiddo?" I felt a lot more comfortable with him now that he was on my turf. Moves had to be delicate but making a place for him in our home felt just fine.

"This looked like food," he said, "so I thought I'd cook it."

"We can do better than that." Sophie and I had stopped at Pohl's on the way to the airport to get him some croissants and I set them out on the table.

"Mom, what if Sophie and Sean had met and not known they were brother and sister?" Luke said between bites of toast. "You read about things like that."

"Are you going to call your parents, Sean? Tell them that you're here safely?" I folded back the newspaper and settled myself in for Saturday morning with all my children home. Maybe we could go out and rake leaves.

"Of course I am."

Sophie came down looking peaked and full of her usual bones. I was glad she'd moved back. She opened the fridge and looked in the freezer. "What happened to my pink mouse?"

"She means mousse, actually," said Luke. "She makes them in popsicle trays and eats them all herself." He put his hand to his mouth and whispered a stagy aside. "I ate it, actually."

Sean got on the phone and tried to call Paris, but there was no answer. He couldn't think where his parents might be—they were always home at this time of day. Sophie pulled her robe over her legs. "Oh, well, I'll have a croissant." Sean got anxious and kept trying the phone call at shorter intervals.

"You could try later," I said.

"No, I'd better try now."

"The wind might come up today, Sean. We could go out on the board." Luke gazed out the window, willing the fog to lift. The sun was a pale yellow break in the mist.

"We've got the shopping to do today, honey. Maybe it could wait."

"Sean can drive, Mom."

Finally, an hour later, he got through to Jean-Paul and Loesic. "*Bonjour. Bonjour. Elle va bien. Vous allez bien?*"

They were fine, he was fine, so we were all fine.

Once the phone call was out of the way, Sean set off for the living room to put on a Mozart tape, came back and ran water for the dishes, turned off the tap, *merde*, he'd missed the beginning, went back to rewind it. Did we have a bike? Did we have a *cinémathèque*? Wasn't it great the way all the houses on the street were different from each other? And how the mountains got really flat just as the sun set, when they'd all been different shapes and shades of blue the minute before? He liked our stove and fridge. They didn't have appliances like that in Europe. What in fact were we going to do that night? We'd have to do a lot every day because he could only stay two weeks, and he had to get thinking about getting some plane reservations because he had to find the cheapest possible way to get to New York so he could go and see Gilbert and Fred, maybe I remembered them from the fête?

"You want to know the cheapest way?" Luke asked.

"The cheapest."

"You know our mountains?"

"I've noticed, yes." His English had sure improved.

"What you do is pick the tallest one you can find, it's got to be in the spring when the rivers have started to run after the snow melts? Then you jump on one of those river rafts, hang on tight and it carries you right down into the States free."

"Good idea." He took Sophie's knife and ladled blackberry jam onto his croissant.

"It's lots of fun, too."

"I'll bet."

"I've got to go to the store, Sean," said Sophie. "You coming?"

"Sure." His face lit up now that she'd asked him to do something with her. But first he turned to Luke. "We're going to go wind-surfing tomorrow, Luke. You're going to teach me, okay?"

"Okay."

"Sophie, Sean, take the dog!"

"He's not a dog," Sophie shouted back up the stairs. "He's a kangaroo."

"Take him anyway."

Just before they left, the two of them climbed out on the balcony up onto the fire escape and, grasping the rungs, leaned way out holding imaginary telescopes, as if they had sighted land.

"Land ho, what?"

"What?"

"What about France?"

"La France est perdue."

"Let's just say she was a charming demoiselle and I wanted to take the opportunity to say sweet things to her."

The next day we were driving along the stretch of Jericho Beach that looks across to the north shore and Bowen Island. We took the long way around past the university to show Sean the inlet and the view of the mountains. We were on our way to my mother's for lunch, which would feature her strawberry glacé pie. She had said she was sure Sean would like it because it was going to be French.

"How is it going to be French?" I had asked.

"It's going to have custard underneath the strawberries. That makes it French."

"Oh."

"Yes, I think Sean will like two things about me. My strawberry pie and my Citroen."

I explained to Sean that the long stretches of sand and rocky beach made it possible to be in this city without seeming to be in a city, if he saw what I meant, going on about the obvious although I knew perfectly well he could see for himself. He was less interested in the travelogue than in how to say "sweet things" in English. It seemed that when he was given information or directions they registered somewhere in him like a sounding, and then he came back and rediscovered them for himself. It wasn't that he didn't appreciate the information, he just had to find it again in his own way.

"Have you ever been to Montreal, Kathleen? I saw this city through a movie of Claude Chabrol, *Les liens du sang*. It looks like a brilliant place." Sophie and Luke were in the back seat, as usual looking out opposite windows. They had always listened to different music in their heads, those two. We had walked along the wide tidal flats at Wreck Beach out to where you could see the cluster of downtown high-rises seeming to float on the water like a mirage, an Isfahan in the sun. It looked as if there were hardly any water that morning between the edge of the flats and the mountains, certainly not enough to float the freighters anchored in the bay. The fog had lifted and the sea gulls wheeled in higher and wider circles. Sailboats scooted before the wind like white arrows and probably in Luke's mind he was on one of them. We sat on barnacled rocks, wiped our feet, put on our shoes and got back in the car, headed up the curved hill past Wreck Beach. I noticed that Sean's travel-weary look was gone.

"Well, it's tricky to say something like 'saying sweet things' in English. We're more likely to say something like 'I was attracted to her.'" I stopped at a corner and signalled.

"Can't you find a better way to say it?"

"Maybe I can. How about something like 'someone I wanted to flirt with'?" We passed the university gardens.

"But in French it doesn't mean I want to flirt with her. What I'm saying is that I wanted to speak *sous-entendus*."

"I guess we don't have an equivalent."

"You can find an image."

We turned the corner at the end of the point where you could see the ocean below between the trees in the forest. I wondered which trail he would like best, which beach.

"Okay, I can find an image, but what I'm trying to say is that in English it's harder to find a casual phrase or image. In French you have more ways of saying these things and it takes out the heat to have more intimacy in the complications of the language. It's so . . . polarized in English. It's either on or off. 'I wanted to say sweet things' is nice but it's more self-conscious; it doesn't have the same ease as the way you say it. To speak *sous-entendus*." Sophie and Luke seemed to have fallen asleep.

"All right." He didn't want to agree with me but he was resigned. "Anyway, I was telling you about this friend I had before Christina, my other friend called Sophie."

"I didn't know you had another Sophie in your life who wasn't our Sophie."

"I had another Sophie in my life." He said this twirling an imaginary moustache in a parody of the melodramatic villain, looking over his shoulder at his sister. She hit him on the arm. He grinned.

"Kathleen, do you know the *points d'ancrage*? When ships arrive in a port, you know, it's thanks to them they stay in this port?"

"You mean a place to anchor?"

"You got it. Well, Gilbert found such a place to anchor in his friend Fred, who is the *new yorkais* I'm going to see when I go there for the first time. For example, in this second life I was trying to tell you about, this Fred who *était assez petit, trapu, très drôle, il avait en plus un charme irrésistible*."

"Very funny with an irresistible charm?"

"Yah, oui, you got it. Squat. Also short. I learned and understood later that he was *à voile et à vapeur*."

"You mean it was all a front?"

"No, that he was a *bisexuel* man."

"A what?"

"*Bisexuel.* You don't have that word? That he was sometimes with a woman and sometimes with a man?"

"Oh, bisexual?"

"Oui, later, *était à voile et à vapeur* is another way to say it. *Leurs chevauchées* were famous in the castle. Did you hear them the night of the fête?"

We drove up the hill. It was hot and glaring and the strips of tar in the road were sticky. Lawns were neatly clipped and the sprinklers turned sedately. "*Leurs chevauchées?* Is that riding?"

"Sure. And it's lovemaking. Do you know that movie *La chevauchée fantastique?* It's an American movie about the riding. You can only say that it is both. On the horse and in the bed. Is this it?"

"This is it. This is Grandma's," said Luke, coming back to life. Driving always made him sleepy and carsick.

We pulled up in front of the neat shuttered house trimmed with white around the door and windows. The begonias stood in rows in the sunken garden and pink geraniums lined two boxes along the brick stairs. Usually the children rushed in ahead of me and waited for Mother to appear with her ritual greeting at the door. This time Sophie waited for Sean and very nicely made the presentation.

"How do you do, Sean." Mother was tanned and slim in a pink gingham dress. Sean leaned over and kissed her on both cheeks, something she wasn't used to, but she smiled nevertheless. At lunch, she was polite and bright. She has poise and will. She put him in Dad's place at the dining room table and even said, "*Passez le beurre.*"

She did not have a picture of Sean in the gallery of grandchildren and honorary grandchildren on the dining room bureau, not because she hadn't been offered one. She said she didn't think it right, out of respect for his being the Richters' son. I also suspected it would be too much for her to have to explain it all to her friends. I watched him spooning cold cucumber soup. I expected he'd noticed and, if so, had handled it well. We had a nice lunch, took the obligatory tour of the garden, made plans for a get-together at the cottage on Bowen Island on Saturday, probably the last of the season. As we were leaving, she looked at Sean and said, "My word, you do look like your mother."

Driving back, Sean was eager to fill me in on what had happened with his friend Christina after I left Paris. His trip to England was, as I could well imagine, somewhat strained what with having just met me for the first time and then travelling so soon with his *anglo-français*. As he approached the British shores, he suffered what he called *une angoisse étouffante*, which is sort of . . . he didn't really know.

"A stifled feeling," explained Sophie from the back. "Also we have to stop at the 7-Eleven and get juice."

"But in the end," he said, "I developed quite a good relationship with the capital of roast beef. Where are we going now?"

"Home."

"Oh, home."

No sooner had we pulled up in front of the house than Luke and Sophie were out of the car and up the stairs. Sean stayed behind to help with the stuff we'd bought on our shopping trip. "The thing is, Kathleen, I don't really have a girl friend right now. It's all over with Christina. I have a problem with relationships. I get too pulled into them . . . Remember with Christina? I wasn't so nice to you after that."

"That was okay."

"Really?"

"Oh, sure."

"No, what I'm ready for, and I have to say this, is to have my sister, to have Sophie. After I met you, I felt more . . . comfortable about her."

"That makes sense." I could tell he was more like me than my other children. Had trouble keeping his perspective, idealized people and read things in. Not at all like Sophie, who always managed to keep an overview even if she didn't let you know it. The sky clouded over with thick dark clouds and it started to rain.

"And you?" he said.

"Oh, me." I was about to get out of the car, but stopped and stared at the dashboard. "I'm not too good at them either, I guess. I'm always trying to accept the fact that I'm . . . by myself. It has to do with the hard part about there being no one there . . . I guess."

I thought he looked sad, but he turned to me and said, "I'm here."

I smiled and gathered up the packages. "I know you are, and it means an awful lot to me, Sean."

We started up the stairs and I decided to risk sounding pedantic. "I've been given a technique for dealing with that feeling of being pulled away into another person, a lover, like you say."

"You have? What is it?" He spun around, his bag

slipping under his arms. All the lights were on, the Pogues on the tape deck and Sophie on the phone. I rested my bag on the newel post.

"Well, when you start feeling yourself being pulled in that way, what you do is take a step backwards—mentally—and say to yourself, who is this person? What are they about? I was told it's an exercise for not letting need interfere with judgement." His look told me it wasn't even a remote possibility.

"Oh, I could never do that."

I sighed and picked up the bags. "No, it's difficult."

After supper he asked to borrow my membership card to the Pacific Cinémathèque so he and Sophie could go to *The Scarlet Empress*. He told Sophie she looked like a true Parisienne in her orange sweater, short black skirt and high heels. She said she liked hooker clothes, enjoyed those shops in Pigalle. She told me later she thought he was more relaxed and funny this time around. "At least he sees the humour in my clothes."

The next day he took the bike and went out to explore. He came back pleased and excited. "This city is surrounded by beaches!"

7

The party for Mother—it was her birthday—and Sean over at the cottage went well in spite of the rain. It's only a ten-minute walk from the wharf to the cottage, so people usually park their cars in Horseshoe Bay, walk on the ferry and arrive at the cottage trailing bits of pine needles and sand onto the linoleum patterned to look like hardwood. We were the only ones who drove our car onto the ferry because we had the wind-surfer with us, strapped to the roof, fin up.

Since it was her birthday, Mother was not supposed to be doing anything, but the minute she arrived she began hauling out old raincoats from the attic cupboard in case people wanted to go for walks. The rain was so fine the grain of the drops was only visible against the dark shape of the trees. The yellow wicker chair sat by the porch railing facing out to sea exactly where I'd left it.

Mother found a pot to put under the leak in the unfinished part of the back porch. Sean was nothing if not schooled in the social graces and immediately doffed his Burberry—he wore a casually tailored silk shirt underneath—and began to pour Seven-Up for the little kids. He took a glass down to my uncle, who was checking the retaining wall he had been building with cement and driftwood.

My sister arrived from the other side of the island in her jeep with the bumper sticker that reads HONK IF YOU LOVE JESUS. She has an open candid face and went up to Sean with the warm curiosity of any aunt at the prospect of seeing her new nephew, home from overseas. My family were all pleased to see him and were soon comfortable with him, perhaps because he looked so much a Haggerty. And Sean handled it well; he was at ease, which put them at ease.

My brother and sister-in-law's two adoptive girls were there as well, looking at the rain-shaped trees. I couldn't help wondering what kinds of questions Sean's being there raised for them. One of my nieces served the cake, but when it was time to blow out the candles, she got mixed up and headed in Sean's direction instead of Mother's. I touched her shoulder and rerouted her just in time. She told me in a whisper she thought Sean was really cute.

My aunt put her leatherette purse down on the kitchen counter, squared her handsome shoulders and took out a French phrase book. With the rain it was cool enough for a fire. I hung a bunch of dried pearly everlasting beside the cardboard seascape reproduction.

Sean and Luke, wearing old running shoes with the toes cut out, went down to the rocky beach below the house and floated the wind-surfer out into the bay. Everyone gathered on the verandah to watch. Luke leaped on the board, bending his knees and pushing down with his heels so the board caught the leverage and shot off. Sean applauded and waded out to join him. He tried to follow Luke's instructions but he had a hard time. The wind was poor and he kept tipping over. Luke suggested they go around to another beach out of sight of the cottage until he got the hang of it, but Sean didn't want to do that. Finally, he got the bar hooped the right way and shoved off into the waves shouting in triumph. The mist lifted and the water reflected a thousand suns. He was underway for a only few minutes before he lost his balance and tipped over again. Luke swam out and they kicked the board back in together. I watched them happily, memorizing the details. I knew I'd have to dole these memories out to myself over and over again.

Later, Sean sat on the railing on the verandah, very relaxed, talking to Sophie. He reached up and traced the line of a branch of dogwood leaning against the house. He liked to be right up close when talking to her, taking her hand and leaning into the conversation. But what about Tim, who was sitting close by? Sophie did her best to divide her attention between the two of them, but it was quite a neck-craning exercise.

My mother, together with my aunt and uncle, walked around the side of the house and discussed the possibility of extending the verandah into a deck and putting a glass door into the old kitchen nook. Likely, Mother wouldn't come back until her birthday next year, when they'd discuss it again. Later she went down to the beach and sat on her rock—hers since she was a girl—with her arms around one knee in the classic bathing beauty pose, grey hairs wisping from her bun, her flamingo polyester pantsuit bright as a salmonberry.

"Next time you come, Sean," she said as she was leaving in my aunt's car, "bring your parents."

The rain continued the next day. I took in the bathing suits that had been almost dry the night before and hung them on the fire screen. For a while that morning, it seemed like the overhanging scrim might just be mist or clouds. The dogwood branches lifted and lowered a few times, and a few ragged patches of blue appeared above the far shore, patches a stranger would take for blue sky. "It looks like it's going to clear up," Sean said.

"No, that's the mountains."

Then it all closed down again. My family's place is a Union Steamships cottage built in the old tongue-and-groove style. It was built, along with others like it on the island, when the steamships were still plying the coast, carrying passengers and freight. Most of the furniture in our cottage had been bought when the island hotel was torn down. There was a trellis at the back door where there was always a honeysuckle, but it never grew because of the shade.

In the afternoon we settled by the fire to go over some of our family history. Sophie dug out her old letters and Sean was banging away on the typewriter, telling us more stories about Pruniers, his *demeure mauresque*, as he called his house, which was so terribly old and had so much history that people couldn't help but be reminded of the *personnages fabuleux* who had lived there in the past. Those tribes who say that people should encounter their deaths in their initiation rites are right, he said. He knew this because the constant encounters he and his friends had with the dead who had lived in the castle before them gave them *l'étincelle essentielle de la connaissance de soi*, that essential spark of self-knowledge, which a person gets from being associated with the death of the person in whose bed they are sleeping.

I looked over his shoulder. "*C'est ainsi que débuta . . .* 'This is,' let me try, 'This is the beginning of their story'?"

"It's a bit like that. It's the beginning of the story of the summers. *La saga des étés.*"

"Saga, we have that."

"So you know then."

"Yes. And *J'atteignais.* What's that word?"

"Reached."

"So now you've reached the age of four and everything's going fine?"

"Right."

It was at this time, he said, that a lot of young people began to come down to Pruniers to help with the restoration, especially after the student riots in 1968. The people who came were often a bit lost and wanted to sort themselves out and find where they wanted to go. They came to Pruniers because—and everyone had to admit this—nothing, absolutely nothing, could be more secure than a combination of Maman and Pruniers.

"Well, yes. Sean, *déblayer*, to remove, to clear away? Is that the verb form of this *déblaiement*, a clearing?"

"Sure."

"And then *enfouir sous des ronces*? Is that meadows?"

"No, it's a sharp, you know, like from a rose?" He was trying to get Sophie to look at him, but she was absorbed in her letters, legs thrown over one of the old flowered armchairs. The tide was half in and half out, exposing the barnacled rocks and ochre sand with blue-shelled mussels. It was still and quiet.

"And *des gravats*, you know, the stones, *La Belle au bois dormant*. Beauty in the woods sleeping."

"What's a *trou*?"

"It's a hole."

"And the sides were like *lézards*? Is that an enamel?"

"No, an animal."

"Oh, like a lizard."

"Yah, you know, in the trees you have a sort of form of lizard? When the plaster is broken you have holes in the wall shaped like, you know, that word you just looked up."

"Fissure. Tell me, Sean, was it fun, all that clearing? Do you remember it all, or do you suppose, maybe, you got in the way a lot?"

"I didn't get in the way. Why would I get in the way? I helped. What I remember is—I told you this—how Maman bought me a wheelbarrow and I came and went with everybody else helping carry out the stones. It's all we did for weeks."

"And so then Maman bought you an igote?" He gave me the dictionary. "Oh, a he-goat. In English we say billy goat. Did you take him in the wheelbarrow as well? You must have. You must have gone back and forth with him in the little wheelbarrow. I can just see you."

"No, Kathleen," he said patiently. "He was too big."

"It wasn't a toy?"

"No, he was real. He was my friend."

"Oh, I didn't realize."

"There's a lot you don't realize," Sophie said, an edge

to her voice. Several gulls, one after the other, dropped straight down onto the rocks. The bay spread wider as the tide started in.

"But there were *quelques moments de crise*, some moments of crisis, that showed me that an adoption is never easy. Because from the beginning of my childrens . . ."

". . . of your childhood?" I said gently.

"Of my childhood, there were people who said things to me and to my parents—people who didn't understand that the emotional problems around adoption are very complicated. Sophie, you translate." He leaned his chair back against the wall.

She picked up the next sheet. "Because, let's see, where are you, oh, down here. Well, the truth is that the closer it seems you get to your parents and the more you think of yourselves as a family that practically has the same blood, which is what you have to do for security, well then the harder it gets to go back and talk about the truth of the person's origins. But if you don't talk about the fact of the adoption or say anything, then the illusion becomes unhealthy, and then the two don't go together. They fight against each other. I used to get the same feeling doing long division when the teacher would say such and such doesn't go. I would think about the contradiction inherent in my situation and it would be like that." She stopped and looked at him at last.

"Well, it was, Sophie. It was like that."

"Yes." She looked back down and resumed reading carefully, taking time between the words.

"In fact, it had only been a few days before this year's fête when I woke up hoping that Christina was going to turn up—I was feeling sad because I wasn't sure if she was coming—but when I looked down from the grenier window early in the morning, I saw Gilbert standing at the door with a mounted deer head under one arm and *un sac à dos démodé*, that is to say an ugly backpack, over the other shoulder. Gilbert had picked up the deer head in London as a joke, and following not far behind Fred and Gilbert was the embarrassed Mickey, the one who always wore a Mickey Mouse T-shirt but in different colours. They burst in, slammed the front door, and Gilbert announced angrily that they had just arrived back in Paris from London exhausted and were about to try to get some sleep when Mickey showed up and confessed that she had told her husband that she was Gilbert's lover—she wasn't, it was just her fantasy. But her husband believed her and was in a rage so she talked them all into catching the next train for Pruniers. They dumped their bags on the table. As usual, they'd stopped in the village for the mail and Gilbert handed Maman a letter that she turned over and then went to the window to read."

I was lost. "This is Mickey, not the Niki I know, right?"

"That's right, Mother." They raised their eyebrows at one another. "She was the one sewing the dress on the dummy that first night, Kathleen."

"Oh, right."

Sophie read on. "So Maman turned back to Gilbert and he looked at her as if to ask what was in the letter. Maman said she would tell him later, because right now what they all needed was to get some sleep. But after that, things got completely crazy because both Fred and the Mickey wanted to make love to Gilbert. After three hours of caresses and shouting and pleadings and paranoia in the library, they compromised and all slept together in one big bed because the Mickey was crying and Gilbert didn't want her to disturb the whole castle. The next day Gilbert decided to prepare his famous *recette du remède contre le chagrin d'amour*. This famous foolproof remedy against the sadness of love was for me, because I was missing Christina, and also for the Mickey. He took squares of black chocolate and melted them in a copper saucepan and then added masses of chestnut cream. He was just getting it ready when the phone rang. He picked up the receiver in one hand, tucked the phone under his chin so he could keep stirring and then called Maman because it was long distance. And well, Kathleen, it was you."

"It was me? That was me then?"

"That's right. That was you, and you know the actual moment when you came, it wasn't the best possible time for me to be dealing with these things because I'd just eaten this diabolical mixture of Gilbert's. The idea is that you get so sick that you forget all about being in love or any problems like that."

"I see."

"And you know, Kathleen, you remember the girl called Pichia who was at the fête? What I remember is that I was always so scared by her dad because he screamed all the time. But then I saw him two years ago and it was so funny because he was short and funny when he screamed and I had always thought he was terrifying."

"And huge?"

"Huge."

I took over from Sophie, translating Sean's words slowly. "And so it was due to Pichia that you felt certain sadnesses? *Chagrins?*"

"Yes."

"The very first time was *un jour tout de go alors que je venais . . .*" I tried not to translate literally and took an intuitive stab. "Are you saying that when you learned about being adopted, you wanted to come to Vancouver . . . right away?"

"No."

"Oh, I'm sorry."

"No, it's all right. But what *'tout de go alors'* means is 'directly.' So look." He moved forward until his knees were under the table. "I'm telling you directly that I was coming to see this girl called Pichia, who took the place of Sophie for me in a way. I'm telling you how she and I had many lovely times together, particularly when we were in the washroom discovering one another's bodies. But as is often the case with the people you love best, the person who was the source of my greatest pleasure was also the source of my greatest sadness. Because one day I told Pichia that whatever she might say, I was further ahead of her because I had two mothers, not just one like she had. But then she said no, you haven't, because your first mother abandoned you and of course that made me cry. Maman came in and told me it wasn't true, that I was never far from your thoughts, Kathleen, and that one day I was going to see you. But you know when you are a child, what is said by a child your own age is stronger than what your mother tells you. Really, the minute I saw your face I knew what Maman had said was right, but at the time, Pichia . . ."

"Flattened him," said Sophie.

"Yes. Do you understand, Kathleen?"

"Yes, of course I understand. It's very understandable." I reached out to touch his shoulder but I was upset and went into the bathroom, where I accidentally broke a glass in the sink. I was picking up the pieces when Sean came in so we could finish up the translation. "What we need to do," he said, "is to take this story further along. After that incident with Pichia, when my parents went out, I always insisted on going with them, wherever they went. They said, in fact they promised, I could sleep in the bedroom with the coats. But one more time I was afraid they would forget me, so instead of staying in there with the coats, I insisted on lying down at their feet."

"So you're telling me that, after that, when your parents went out to friends for dinner you went with them and slept under their feet at the table?"

"That's right. And it was really good. That was a good place to sleep."

"Oh, Sean."

"No, Kathleen, really. It was a good place to sleep."

The next night while I was washing my hair at the kitchen sink, Sophie decided to take issue with the way Sean had described Jean-Paul's role in the war.

"Don't you think that the way you painted him is a trifle misleading?"

"In that?"

"In that the reason he escaped and went to France was because the German army was going to send them to Russia and he didn't want to go. It was only later that he had any politics around any of this. He was a kid, he was only sixteen. What did he know about any of it?"

"That's not true, Sophie."

"It is true, he told me himself."

"He did a lot of important work in the war. I know more about it than you do."

"I'm aware of that, but it wasn't until later."

"Probably you're both right," I suggested. I bent over the sink to wait for the conditioner to set.

"Probably we aren't, but never mind."

"What I'd like to know is how he went back into the German army. Did he just go back and say, hi guys, or what?"

"Hardly, Mother. He went back with a different identity, of course. That's how they did it."

"I see." I stood up with the towel wrapped around my head.

"Do you know electricity, Kathleen, when it's kind of *étincelle*, sending out sparks like a *court-circuit*?" Sean seemed to be needing to control the conversation. He'd obviously had enough of that subject and wanted to go on to something else.

"Sort of."

"Well, it was from this sort of electricity that someone came out of obscurity with a kind of brilliance for me. And that was Gilbert. He was the one who knows all about my *insécurités*, my fears, my *lâchetés* . . ." It seemed to mean so much to him that I appreciated the qualities of his various friends.

"*Insécurités*, is that like fears?" I sat down with them, rubbing my hair with the towel.

"Yes, it's like fears but not like cowardices." A bee was bouncing against the window and Luke, with a piece of cardboard and a glass, was tracking it, trying to slip the cardboard under the bee and the glass on top.

"And my sadnesses. He's the one who understands that it's cowardice behind certain acts of mine that appear to be brave. And that my real acts of courage are invisible to anyone else but me. Remember at the fête, when you were having a difficult time at the table because the conversation was going too fast for you and you couldn't keep up so you went upstairs? He was just then trying to use all the strength of his words and the gentleness of his feelings to help me understand that will is the most important thing in the world. Not will by itself but will combined with *l'exigence*."

"That's ridiculous," said Sophie. "He doesn't think that."

"I said only if it's combined with *l'exigence*." He was near tears.

"What's *exigence*? Exigency?"

"Sure."

"Did he go to a Jesuit school by any chance?" Sophie asked.

"I don't know. The point is what he was telling me all the time is that mediocrity is shit, and it will always be shit. And meanwhile *la beauté*, the beauty, the essence of beauty, not beauty like you are beautiful but the kind of beauty that means integrity, that kind of beauty, will go on elsewhere and you will miss its exigency. Beauty is exhausting to be and to do, and in the future it will be the same." Sophie still looked skeptical.

"So what he was saying," I tried my hand, "was that the line of least resistance is comfortable, but choosing the harder way is ultimately more . . ."

"Mom, open the door. Open the door, I've got the bee. Quick."

Sean opened the back door. Luke slid the cardboard off the glass and the bee zoomed off.

"Yah, that's right." Sean looked exhausted. "And when Gilbert had something to tell me about my weakness, he said, you are wrong in what you are doing and he is right."

He slumped back on the chair and sighed.

Later I walked to the wharf with Luke who was dribbling a soccer ball. The ferry was coming in. The rain had stopped, although some puddles filled up beside the posts in the back of the house. A boat engine gargled in the bay. The sun reappeared, brightening the rocks a tone to ochre. The wild rose was almost finished for the year, and I watched a single petal spinning around on a strand of cobweb.

I had been working on a sketch of Luke and Sean that morning, messing with pale blue watercolour and then washing on a layer of water with no colour at all. Tiny crabs scurried around the bottoms of small puddles on the beach. Far away, a gull turned over, hardened into view against the dark hill for a moment, then disappeared into the whitecaps. We sat on a grassy slope above the harbour—the ferry was on its way but had dropped out of sight momentarily behind the south side of the cove. Visitors often became anxious when this happened, thinking they had misread the schedule. A woman in the ferry line-up asked us when the boat was due. "Don't worry," I told her. "It's there, you just can't see it. You'll see it in a few minutes."

Luke muttered, but under his breath, yanked out a bunch of grass and heaved it down the bank. Sure enough, the ferry reappeared, lurching back and forth, getting ready, as usual, to smash up against the ferry slip. Then we heard a commotion up at our side of the cove and all at once a deer bounded out of the forest onto the beach with our dog hard on its heels. It crashed into the water, antlers erect, and began to swim for the opposite shore. It was on a direct collision course with the ferry. We saw Sean down at the edge of the water yelling at the dog to come back. The dog was gaining on the deer, trying to climb on its back.

"Oh, Jesus," said Luke, just as he had the previous spring when he and I were camping up on Saginaw Lake and had made the mistake of forgetting to dig up and turn over the roots of our fire after we put it out. The ground was peaty where we camped. I thought we had put the fire out safely, but it travelled underground while we slept and suddenly the whole arc of the canoe lit up like a torch. We burst out of the tent, raced down the slope, picked up the canoe and hurled it into the lake. Luckily, Luke had flipped the canoe on its side just before we turned in, so the hole from the fire was limited to the area above the water line. We were miles up the lake and there was no road back.

Luke and I raced down under the wharf, scrambling along the rocks to where Sean was watching the deer, which was being squeezed by a German shepherd trying to mount it from the rear and the ferry threatening to hit it broadside from the front.

"GET BACK HERE!" Luke hollered. Astonishingly, the dog obeyed. He turned around in a wide semicircle, nosing himself back to the beach, climbed out on shore and shook himself as if nothing had happened. Luke smacked him across the nose, grabbed him by the collar and led him back to the cottage. Meanwhile, the deer continued its stately pace in the water. The people waiting for the ferry started cheering for the deer to swim faster, as the ferry was closing in. The deer just made it, barely crossing the boat's oncoming path in time, and surfed on the wake to the opposite shore. Then it climbed calmly out of the water and walked sedately off into the bushes. If the ferry hadn't swerved off course earlier to miss a pleasure boat, the deer wouldn't have made it. I expected the RCMP to show up that evening—dogs on Bowen are not allowed to chase deer.

"He's just a dog," Luke told Sean, standing out by the back porch. "It's instinct. He doesn't know any better. People want the deer off the point anyway. They eat all the gardens. Look at this," pointing to the hydrangeas. "People have to put these stupid nets over everything."

Sean was still white-faced, scared. "That's not the point, Luke."

"Mom, come here. Sean's acting as if he's the only one who's upset. Look at poor Max." Max was cowering under the house. Poor Max, indeed.

"The dog," said Sean, "is only acting like he always does. At home he goes sideways down the stairs in front of me on purpose to trip me."

"He doesn't do that on purpose. That's just the way he walks."

"Sure," said Sean and went up to my brother's old room to be alone for a while.

"Luke," I said, "we may be in serious trouble about this. They shoot dogs who chase deer on the island."

"Fine, then I'm going home on the next ferry. And I'm taking Max with me."

"I don't want you staying by yourself."

"Kim's downstairs."

"We don't know if she's home tonight."

"Sophie will come with me."

I sighed. "Well, maybe we should all go back."

At this point, Tim and Sophie took it upon themselves to calm everybody down. The dog hadn't killed the deer; the deer was still alive. The deer had had a nice swim. We might even consider that perhaps Luke had a point when he said that the residents on this side would be glad the deer had migrated, and there were no houses on the other side. If we lived here there would be a problem because the dog would have to be tied up all day but, as they understood it, we would be leaving tomorrow, wasn't that correct? So why didn't we all just settle down and roast some marshmallows as we had planned and have a pleasant evening? Yes, they knew there was a rule against chasing deer, but there was no rule about swimming after deer. So what if that was a stupid rationalization? In fact, probably no one would show up. As it turned out, they were right: no one did.

Sean came back downstairs and, as he walked across the living room, reached out and put his hand on Luke's shoulder where he sat in a chair by the fire reading. Tim and Sophie were on the porch. Luke went to bed, leaving Sean and me alone by the fire. I thought about that night on Saginaw Lake; it was a miracle that I had woken up in time. Luke had gone right back to sleep but I'd sat up the rest of the night, pouring potfuls of lake water onto the remains of the fire, unaccountably thinking about Loesic, looking at the moon and calculating what to leave behind, that is, if the boat would float at all.

Sean picked up the hollow brass poker, sighted down it, blew on the fire through it and got a mouthful of ash. "What are you thinking about, Kathleen?"

I told him about our excursion up to Saginaw that was supposed to have been a four-day trip. Because of the fire, the only thing we could do was go home, get the canoe repaired and then go back later. You fall off a horse, you get back on. And the second time we took duct tape.

"And you left the dog at home the second time too?"

"How did you know?"

He smiled, put another piece of wood on the fire and picked up some pamphlets that were on the table. They were part of an effort on my great-aunt's part to trace our family tree and history back to its roots in Ireland. He leafed through the old pictures of relatives on their farms in Ontario and Saskatchewan. I noticed he was looking at a bookmark in one of the pamphlets and suddenly remembered that many years before the invitation had arrived, I had been looking through the same pamphlet and had written "Sean Haggerty Richter" on the bookmark because I had always regretted not giving Sean my name. I wondered if he'd seen it.

"They were mostly farmers, then," he said, "these Haggertys."

"They were. Most of the Irish settlers who originally came out were labourers. On the other side, too. You have French blood there. My mother's mother was a Cantelon."

"Then maybe I could be French and Canadian."

"It's been done before, apparently."

He picked up the poker and turned the log on its back.

The next morning he went out to the end of the rocky outcrop on the beach and sat on the farthest boulder he could find. I took some coffee out to him, wading through the barnacles and mussel shells in the running shoes he had worn yesterday. The dog followed.

"Oh, you," he said to the dog. He'd almost forgiven him.

Together we watched as what looked like a small block of wood floating on the surface suddenly dove underwater. It was an auklet. They're not good flyers; they crash into things and make almost human cries and moans because they can't see where they're going.

"I've been looking for a place like this for a long time," he said finally. This was a more sober, more mature side of him I was seeing today. "I don't know quite how to put it, but for me the only phrase I can think of is virgin of images. Back in France every piece of ground has a thousand stories already." I looked at him carefully.

"Sean, would you like to go in there, further behind those mountains? We could go next weekend."

"Sure. Sure I would."

"Well then, let's do it. It can be arranged."

8

After dinner at the Faculty Club a couple of nights later, my friend from the French department, Terry Mahler, his son, Jim, Sean and I went to see Sophie and her pal Tami in their new group, The Wanabees. They were playing at a club behind the green neon of Granville Street. Strobe lights flashed on their sequined dresses and hot shoulders as they whipped their streaked blonde hair back and forth, flipping it over their heads and back. Between sets, Terry regaled us with stories about his last trip to France, which had included a visit to the grave of Jim Morrison at the famous Père Lachaise cemetery. Three or four sad women had been gathered around the little mausoleum whose walls featured inspirational graffiti such as "Jim Morrison forever" and "Jim Morrison's music will never die." There was also a revisionist message: "Now Jim Morrison stinks just like all the rest." Sean laughed and said it was clear from that story that Dr. Mahler truly understood French culture.

Sean and Jim Mahler went off together and Terry went to the bar to get himself a drink. I noticed Sophie's friend

Rosebud sashaying between the tables. The stage was a wild array of lights and flashing drumsticks. Then all of a sudden Sophie showed up and plunked herself down beside me and helped herself to my drink.

"For god's sake, Mother, what am I supposed to do about Sean? He's following me around like a sulky boy. What's he doing confusing himself with my boyfriend, making me jump through hoops like this? He's my *brother*. I mean, he's really out of line."

"I wonder if part of it might be cultural?"

But she wasn't having any of it. "Oh, come on, Mother. We can't say give the guy a break because he's French. He has a duty to me to be mature and normal. He knows he's out of line. I mean he knows."

"Is that it?"

"Of course that's it. There's nothing romantic about this. It's fucked up. Every time I try, I can't do things right, I blow it. I've put more into this than anybody. I've been, like, really hospitable and I don't know what he wants. Maybe it's less primal or something for Sean to use me, I don't know." She was near tears. "It's not my fault. I was only a little kid when all this happened."

"Oh, Sophie, don't think I don't know it." I reached over and took her hand. "You've been in an impossible position all along. I shouldn't have let you go to France. It was too much of a burden. I didn't think it through sufficiently. I'm sorry, I really am."

"Why didn't you come home?"

"How do you mean?"

"When Sean was born. Why didn't you come home?"

"I'd come home to have you, I told you that. I'd gone

back against everyone's advice so you would have your dad and we would be together, and I had to prove to my family we could make it. I couldn't do it again."

"You mean Andrew left when you were having me as well?"

"Let's just say he wasn't around a lot."

"That's what you've always said, that he was working or something."

"Well, he was."

"Boy, you really are a sucker for punishment, aren't you?" She was calmer now. "Maybe if I'd been more disillusioned before I went to France, it would have helped. It worked when I was little, telling it like a story. But I have this guilt, I keep thinking I have to fix things. And I can't do it." She looked so distressed.

"Sophie, if I'd known for sure that Sean was Andrew's baby I'd have held onto him for dear life." She looked up at me, then down at her drink again.

"That makes me feel better, oddly enough. It worked out for them, for the Richters, but you know, it's what you did too, Mom. Frankly, I wish we'd been together. You could have managed. People would have helped you. Then I would have had my brother."

"I know that."

"Why didn't you get a blood test for Sean? You've just never used any logic, have you? Was logic a dirty word in the sixties or something?"

Terry returned with his drink and another for me. "Anyway, just tell him to back off, will you? I have Tim to think of as well." She flicked her heels and disappeared into the crowd.

"Problems?" he asked.

"Oh, you know, nothing that I shouldn't have antici-pated." He handed me the Scotch. "Thanks."

"I wish I could stay, but it's late. I have to go home."

"I know. Good night, Terry, and thanks."

After he left—Jim stayed on, having, it appeared, con-nected up with various friends—Sean came back, his face strained and white. "Where's Sophie?" I jerked my thumb. He stared in the direction I pointed, sat down and put his head down on his arms. "What am I going to do about Sophie?"

"Nothing. Don't do anything."

"I can't do nothing. She told me I was being disgust-ing." He covered his face.

"She doesn't mean it."

"But that's what she *said*."

Then, just as abruptly, he left. I tried to follow but couldn't find him on the street, or up the block, so I went back to where the car was parked. He was trying to open the car doors even though he could see they were locked. I put my arms around him and he put his head down on my shoulder.

"She . . . how can she say that? She's my sister. I wanted . . . I just wanted to be close to her . . ." He leaned up against the side of the car, smashed his fist on the roof. "And I can't talk English any more. It's like a game to me. I need Sophie. At least she speaks French."

"Sean, Sophie isn't you. It's because you've had to think about her for so long without knowing her that it's hard to sort out. And she's . . . different from the way you imagine her, I think." When I said that I heard the flat voice of the person who'd botched up both their lives.

This is not all my fault. "Do you remember what we were talking about the other day? This is exactly the kind of situation I meant, where you can try, just try, to step back and say to yourself, who is this girl, what is she about? She's more reserved, believe me."

He was still leaning on the top of the car, his face buried in his arms. Then he looked up and said, "She isn't, you know."

"Let's just take a walk around the block." We walked over to the law courts and around the fountain.

"She likes all these clothes of whores. Fishnet stockings, she's not inhibited about that."

"That's her public role."

"What about tomorrow? I'll have to phone her and explain. Is she staying at Tim's tonight or what?"

"How about just giving her a bit of time? I know her pretty well. She'll be back."

He tried again. "What about when we drive to Seattle?"

"When we drive to Seattle it will be fine. Just step back a little and observe. Try it."

"I can do that."

"I know you can." I hesitated a moment, then said it anyway. I sounded so trite with these life-skill aphorisms, a mother deprived of her role trying awkwardly to make up for it, but I had nothing to lose.

"Brothers and sisters here are not quite so . . . *tête à tête.* They don't touch each other so much in Canada."

"Really?" He was astonished. "I can sure see why people are so crazy about France."

The next morning we sat on a bench on the deck of the Langdale ferry. Reaches of land appeared and disappeared into the fjord. Everyone, with the exception of Luke, was raw from the night before and hung over too. Sophie had her mirror out and was coating her face with sunscreen.

"Mom, I've been thinking about when we drive Sean to Seattle to catch his plane." Sean and Luke were on one side of me, she was on the other. "Does Sean have a visa for the States?"

"Of course Sean has a visa for the States." I looked back and forth between them.

"So what are we going to tell them at the border?"

"Why should we worry about that?" said Sean. "For administrative purposes I'm not related to you."

"You'd better wear dark sunglasses, then, Mom, that's all I can say." She picked up her purse and headed for the cafeteria. ("Of course I'm coming," she had told me when I called her that morning. "You can't get rid of me that easily.")

"You want to come and play video games?" Luke asked Sean, holding his hand out to me for quarters.

"Thanks, Luke, I think I'll just sit here with your mother, okay?"

"Okay."

We were heading up the coast to a piece of forest on the Sechelt peninsula I had bought a few years back with a group of friends, partly in the hopes my children might all get together someday and build themselves a house. I kept going up to have a look at it and then driving home again. Once the ferry rounds Hood Point, the city disappears and the darker islands bulk into view. The wind and salt air fill your lungs; the sense of space expands back into the wilderness and silence. Unfortunately, within minutes of leaving the ferry at Langdale, you're confronted with a concrete and plastic mall and the drag strip lining the highway. I always felt I'd come an awfully long way to escape just that. The two ends of the peninsula are connected by a long highway with dirt road tributaries. You have to turn off and follow them a ways to find the shaded herb farms and spreading glass-and-wood cabins.

On the way to the rough cabin that was already on the land and which all the land owners now share, Sean sat in the back with Luke, resting his chin on the back seat between me and Sophie. We zigzagged up the hill behind the ferry slip. He leaned forward and reached between us to turn on the radio. "What's this terrible dusty place?"

"It's the mall."

"What's the matter with the mall?" Luke, of course.

Sean fiddled with the radio dial. "You know, Kathleen, I was surprised you didn't go home with Dr. Mahler last night. He is so nice and you like each other . . ."

"Dr. Mahler is married, Sean."

"What difference does that make?"

"In Canada it makes a lot of difference." Sophie glared at him.

Sean caught my eye in the rearview mirror. A few miles later we got a sense of the forest again, then turned left into a driveway, the car ducking under the overhanging hemlock and salmonberry bushes all down the lane, which opened onto a clearing where the cabin was located. We piled out of the car dragging sleeping bags, coolers and knapsacks. A couple of mice were caught in the traps I'd left. Sean didn't mind being the one to sleep on a foamie on the kitchen floor. Sophie and I would take the bunk. Luke liked me to back the car up so the hatchback opened onto the deck; he liked to sleep in the back of the station wagon so he could listen to the radio.

The place where I planned to build was even deeper in the woods. We'd have to put a road in and I figured the trees we'd take down would pay for the backhoe and driver. In the morning Sophie woke up bright and cheery, and, after breakfast, Sean and Sophie and I pulled on gum boots and stomped along the muddy trail back into the skunk cabbages. Our site was down a logging slide, around the ocean side of a hill, through another trail and around a corner of slash. (Luke stayed behind so he could practise driving the car around the circular driveway. It's okay without a licence, he said, when it's on your own property.)

Sean and Sophie didn't want to go any farther and in-sisted that where they stood would be the house site. They started hacking away at a dwarf hemlock that barely came up to their knees. I pushed on, scrambled up a rock, slipped on the moss, crawled up and over the edge of the boulder and found the marker tied with a piece of pink ribbon.

"Hey, you kids," I shouted. "You're in the wrong place. It's over here." They protested—I couldn't possibly be right, their place was better, but finally with great sighs and mock protests they trudged and clambered up through the trees hollering and sliding, coming up behind me to look over my shoulder at the uncleared possibili-ties.

"I do think you might have picked somewhere a little more out of the way," said Sean.

The next day we talked about taking a trip to Ruby Lake. It was too hot; who wanted to drive way up to

Ruby Lake on a hot day like that? Sean did, that's who. Why didn't we just go to Sandy Beach? Finally, Sophie offered to go with Luke to Sandy Beach, so we dropped them off along with the picnic basket and thermos. Then Sean and I drove back up the hill and turned onto the highway heading for Ruby Lake.

"So how did I do?" he said.

"You did great."

We passed the sawmill, then curved around the turns on the other side of Sechelt where the arteries of red arbutus grew down the slope near the rocks. Some of the hills had wide slashes and clear-cut scars. Sean craned his neck, trying to see the tops of the hills that enclosed us on both sides. We peered between the mountains as we passed through an area scarred by fire; the hard blackened stumps stuck up jagged along the rough jaw of the ridge. Sean moved closer to me and looked back over his shoulder as we rode into greener country.

"I meant to ask you, what's happening about your military service, Sean?"

"I'm not going to do it. I'm going to try for conscientious objector status."

"Is that difficult?"

"It might be. I'd have to do a year's community service. The other alternative would be to try to convince them I'm mad."

"But they must be used to that. They wouldn't be easily fooled."

"Apparently, you have to drink a lot of wine and a lot of coffee combined. They say it works."

"So you don't want to be a soldier?"

"I don't want to be a soldier."

"You don't think France needs to have an army?"

"I do in a way but I don't want to be conscripted."

"I see."

We broke onto a straight stretch and passed the lone hill where I had gone climbing the weekend I was trying to decide whether or not to go to France. I had been told it was a sacred place to the aboriginal people who live in the area. I remembered climbing hard for an hour and, when I arrived at the top, making my way to the side of the hill that overlooks a small lake. I sat down but felt nothing special about the place, no feeling of vigil. I was just sitting on a hill overlooking a lake. Disappointed, I started back down the trail. Then, as I was passing a particularly large rock, I saw what looked like an entranceway between two tall trees, a vein almost, into another area of the peak. I pulled back a branch, ducked under and stepped over what looked like a rooted collarbone. Large pieces of stone had broken away so the hill could fall back to the side and down into the valley. The silence was vast and there was a view of the mountains all around me. The small hill where I'd been sitting on the other side of the rise seemed sliced away, as if it had fallen into the lake. I slipped once and found myself trying to scramble back up the hill, grabbing onto lichen and roots. I made it but felt panicky; the harder I scrambled, the steeper the hill became. When I regained my footing, I saw what I hadn't been able to see before—a series of oblong- shaped stones placed more or less equidistant from each other circling over the hill and back around the curve out of sight of the lake. I picked up a stone that was off by itself some distance away, thinking to add it to the ring. But I realized that such a gesture had to be earned by belonging and by spending several hungry sleepless nights there. The only altar on the mountainside was not mine. I put the stone back down where I had found it and left.

"Glisso Gellata, that's who I was trying to remember."

"Who's that?"

"The druidess of fire Maman was telling me about. I was trying to think who it was when we were at Bowen."

At the lakeside café we pulled up at a log marking the parking area, ordered hamburgers and french fries from a window hatch and took the paper baskets to a rusty table on the deck. A runty willow trailed its branches in the slick water. A couple of swans paddled over; they looked hollow, like meringues.

"Tell me, Sean, is Loesic still as depressed in Paris as she was?"

"She is, you know. It's because it's all Papa's show in Paris. He works like a madman but Maman more or less stays in the background. At Pruniers, it's the other way around, but they don't get as much time down there."

"I thought he was supposed to be slowing down."

"He is, but he doesn't do it. We try to make him, and it makes a lot of tension among us, but it's tension that gets the motor started after all. It was a compromise that worked for a while, but they needed a change. We had one idea but it didn't work out." He folded his paper plate in half and flattened it. We fed pieces of hamburger bun to the swans.

We left the café and drove high up around the lake. Dust from the gravel road billowed behind us and we rolled up the windows. The wide cliff dropped straight down to the large warm lake. From up there, the depths were darker, more inviting.

"I guess the truth, when you think about it, is that Papa is better physically but psychologically *il était meurtri*." Sean had to thumb through the well-worn dictionary. "Bruised."

"I guess he's not used to taking it easy."

"No, and you know, I haven't told you the whole story about Gilbert. What happened was that Fred, you remember Fred, he spent one whole year lost, *perdu dans l'homosexualité, le sexe, la baise à outrance . . .*"

"What's that?"

"I don't want to translate it."

"Why not?"

"I just don't. The important thing that I haven't told you is that Gilbert contracted *les germes maladifs* and he's going to die of that terrible sickness in four letters. What do you say, a four-letter word?"

"You mean AIDS? Gilbert has AIDS?"

He sucked his lips. "Yes."

"When did you find out?"

"Just before I came."

"Oh, Sean. That's terrible. I had no idea. So that's why you're going to New York?"

"That's why I'm going to New York."

"Are they both there?"

"Yes."

"Loesic and Jean-Paul must be really upset."

"They are."

We parked at the pull-off by the edge of the bank. "Do you still feel like going down for a swim or shall we skip it? Maybe we should skip it."

"No, let's go." He sat grim-faced for a few moments, then reached into his leather bag and took out some much-folded maps and folders. I leaned my arms on the steering wheel.

"The terrible part is that Gilbert is the one who was faithful and he's the one who's going to die now. Fred isn't sick at all yet." He looked at the map he had unfolded, seeming to try to get his mind off the subject. "Are we going to take another ferry and drive down there?" He pointed to Vancouver Island on the map.

"Well, no, we can't. It would take too long. It would take almost a day to drive back down the island."

"You're kidding?"

"Vancouver Island is a third the size of Britain."

"You must be joking."

"Have they given him any idea, do you know how long he has?"

"I don't think so, no."

We got out and climbed down the chunks of avalanche-loosened stones. They were covered with moss so old they must have fallen down before the road was cut through. We had to jump from one rock to the next and finally slid down to the edge of the lake. We heard a wild caw in the distance. The light shafted low across the water. Sean walked behind some rocks to a stand of arbutus and looked up at the hillside where he thought no one had ever lived, he said. He came back and sat down. The stillness was huge and empty.

"I'm going to have to bring my parents out here one day."

"Wouldn't that be something?"

"Yes, it would."

He turned on his back and rested his cheek on the warm rock. The sun was warm and hazy, light shimmering in the soft air.

"Do you know, Kathleen, after you left this summer the nights at Pruniers were exceptionally starry and even then Gilbert was talking about death. And Marie-Claire. Do you remember her? Her husband just died too, it's been like the year of deaths. They were together forty years, they made marionettes. You remember the puppets that hung over my cradle, the little Mountie and the Indian with *le pied noir*? They made those. And Maman's favourite brother drowned, he was a Breton fisherman and he drowned trying to save a friend who couldn't swim, so I lost my favourite uncle and Jean-Paul lost his favourite brother-in-law. Gilbert used to say that deaths are only apparent endings, that really they're opening to something else. Like the windows opening to make it possible for me to come on this trip."

"Tell me, Sean, do you know whatever happened to Niki?"

"No, I don't. I only met her once. She was very weak, very fragile and completely lost in her research of her father. She must be an ambiguous character for you, Kathleen."

"She is. Did she ever find him?"

"Oh, she found him, but he wasn't kind and he wasn't interesting and he couldn't understand how she could have wasted her life looking for him."

"Poor Niki. Do you know where?"

"No, I don't. We lost touch with her. She came to Pruniers once, but then she didn't come any more. I think it was because Jean-Paul wanted to make love with her.

She couldn't understand that. Maman tried to talk to her about it."

"Maman tried to talk to her?"

"*Oui.*"

I shook my head.

"I've had a wonderful time, you know. I've only had one serious disappointment."

"What's that?"

"That Haida is married."

I smiled. "So it goes, eh?"

"Do you think she'd mind?"

"Are you kidding?"

He turned on his back again, smiling. The clouds divided, and when the sun went behind one, its edges lit up. A thread spun from an airplane stretched diagonally across the sky. I turned on my side and looked at him. "Maybe it was Singapore where she found him."

"Maybe."

"Tell me, which of the three characters in the script you were writing ended up being the most interesting to you?"

"Which three are those?"

"The one looking at the picture in the gallery or the woman standing up gripping the hair or the one whose body was lost?"

"All of them. Each of them."

I began to drift off, half asleep.

"I guess you know that Niki took a lot of drugs, even at Bouchauds," he asked.

"No, I didn't know that."

"That was another reason she faded away."

"Sean, Gilbert and Fred, are they both going to stay in New York? I don't like to think of you staying too long there. Don't stay too long, okay?"

"Okay."

I was thirsty and wished I'd thought to bring something to drink. "Ice cubes in a glass jar, wouldn't that be nice?"

"Sure, but we don't have any."

We were silent for a while. Then he said, "I brought some oranges."

"You did? Great."

He reached over and touched my hair. "So, are you going to get us the oranges?"

"Where are they?"

"Over in my bag."

"Why don't you get them?"

"It's your turn."

"Oh, okay."

I walked over to where his knapsack—sac à dos—hung in the arbutus tree, lifted up the flap, reached in for the oranges and tossed them to him, one at a time. In the knapsack I saw a well-worn book, *A Delicate Wilderness*. I'd forgotten all about that book. There were some maps of B.C. and several brochures in French that were also worn; like the invitation, which I'd carried around with me since I got it, the folds were almost slit through. I sat down beside him and peeled my orange.

"Time for a swim?"

"Why not?"

I waded out into the lake and struck a hard overarm into the dark water and, in the middle, turned over to backstroke the rest of the way. Sean squatted on the shore. Then he stood up and headed into the water, swimming as hard as he could, turning his head from side to side above the water. We swam until we were in the middle of the lake and could look back and see the tops of the trees touching the sky. On the far side of the lake I hauled myself out and ran up and down to get dry. Sean came out of the water behind me. He cut his toe on a stone, hopped up beside me, squeezing the cut together, trying to lean over and suck it, but he couldn't quite reach. I sat down beside him, leaned my cheek on my knee and turned to him slowly.

"I have to ask you something, Sean. It's been on my mind since we got here. Were you and your parents planning to come out here . . . one day? Was that the plan?"

"Yes," he said, not at all surprised. "It's always been the plan. We talked about it the way you would, oh, I don't know. People teased us, brought us funny presents. Maman had a Canadian brochure with a picture of a deer on it so, as a joke, Gilbert and Fred brought us that mounted deer head, the one in the hall at Pruniers . . ."

"When was that going to be?"

"After the fête."

We drove back to town slowly. On the ferry we sat on the same bench but this time it faced the other shore. Sean touched my cheek with his knuckle.

"But it was a good time this way, you know, Kathleen. It's been an important time for us. I'm glad you came and got me."

"Oh, I hope so, Sean. I really hope so."

The next morning, before we left for Seattle, I went up and knocked on the door of his room. He was rolling a last sheet of paper into the typewriter.

"You ready to go?"

"Pretty much."

"This is your room, you know, whenever you want. And Jean-Paul and Loesic can have my room when you all come back."

"That's good."

When I went back upstairs to make sure he hadn't forgotten anything, I found the note he had left in the typewriter. *Thanks very much for this trip, Mother. Love, Sean Haggerty Richter.*

Acknowledgements

This book could not have been written without the help of my three children, Justine, Thomas and Eli. Credit is due to Justine for her efforts on behalf of the family, and for permission to use Sophie's letters, to Thomas for his kindness in sharing personal reminiscences and to Eli for his help in sustaining the project.

The work as a whole, to say nothing of the story itself, owes as much to Thomas's parents, Paul and You-You.

Thanks are also due to the many relatives, friends and associates who contributed support and advice along the way: Irene Haggerty, Michael Haggerty, Sharon Haggerty, Robin Pretious, Herb Pretious, Kim Kamimura, Rob Sanders, Burna Barron, Frank Oliver, Denise Bukowski, Maureen Fitzgerald, Beth Slocum, Barbara Seaman, Kris Glen, Claudia MacDonald, Jim Wong-Chu, Ann Munro, Jane Munro, Marguerite Chiarenza, Larry Bongie, David Gibbons, Judith Klang, Alison Ludditt, Rick Friesen and, most especially, my editors, Bob Amussen and Barbara Pulling. I am indebted as well to Dr. H. David Kirk for his writings on adoption.

While *The Invitation* is a true story, it is not a documentary but a memory. Persona names have been used throughout as windows from which to view character. I have also condensed or collapsed certain events to serve the needs of the narrative. My thanks to family members for bearing with these liberties.

I would also like to express my appreciation to the Canada Council for their financial support.

JOAN HAGGERTY was born and raised in Vancouver, British Columbia. From 1962 to 1972, she lived and wrote in England, Spain and New York City. She now makes her home in Vancouver and in a small town in northern B.C., where she works as a high school teacher.

Joan Haggerty's two previous books are *Please Miss, Can I Play God?*, a documentary about her experiences teaching child drama in London, England, and the critically acclaimed *Daughters of the Moon*, a novel told from the point of view of a woman in labour.